The
86
Biggest
Lies on
Wall Street

John R. Talbott

Seven Stories Press

NEW YORK

Seven Stories Press
140 Watts Street
New York, NY 10013
www.sevenstories.com

In Canada: Publishers Group Canada, 559 College Street, Suite 402, Toronto, ON M6G 1A9

In the UK: Turnaround Publisher Services Ltd., Unit 3, Olympia Trading Estate, Coburg Road, Wood Green, London N22 6TZ

In Australia: Palgrave Macmillan, 15–19 Claremont Street, South Yarra, VIC 3141

College professors may order examination copies of Seven Stories Press titles for a free six-month trial period. To order, visit www.sevenstories.com/textbook or send a fax on school letterhead to (212) 226-1411.

Book design by Jon Gilbert

Library of Congress Cataloging-in-Publication Data

Talbott, John R., 1955-
The 86 biggest lies on Wall Street / John R. Talbott.
  p. cm.
ISBN 978-1-58322-887-6 (hardcover)
  1. Investments--United States. 2. Financial crises--United States. 3. United States--Economic conditions--2001- I. Title. II. Title: Eighty-six biggest lies on Wall Street.
HG4910.T357 2009
332.60973--dc22

                              2009007951

Printed in the USA

9 8 7 6 5 4 3 2 1

Ye shall know the truth, and the truth shall make you free.

John 8:32

The truth that makes men free is for the most part the truth which men prefer not to hear.

Herbert Agar

False words are not only evil in themselves, but they infect the soul with evil.

Plato (427 B.C.–347 B.C.), *Dialogues, Phaedo*

Ambition drove many men to become false; to have one thought locked in the breast, another ready on the tongue.

Sallust (86 B.C.–34 B.C.), *The War with Catiline*

All truth passes through three stages. First, it is ridiculed. Second, it is violently opposed. Third, it is accepted as being self-evident.

Arthur Schopenhauer (1788–1860)

Chase after truth like hell and you'll free yourself, even though you never touch its coat-tails.

Clarence Darrow (1857–1938)

This book is dedicated to my mother, Agnes, who instilled in me a desire to seek the truth, and to my publisher, Dan, who must have been similarly inspired by his parents.

Contents

THE 86 BIGGEST LIES ON WALL STREET   x

INTRODUCTION   I

CHAPTER I   Lies About What Caused This Mess   15

CHAPTER 2   Lies About How to End the Crisis   45

CHAPTER 3   Investment Strategy Lies   63

CHAPTER 4   Stock Investing Lies   83

CHAPTER 5   Bond Investing Lies   103

CHAPTER 6   Lies About Other Investments   115

CHAPTER 7   Lies in Economics   131

CHAPTER 8   Lies in Finance   157

CHAPTER 9   Lies About the Global Economy   167

CHAPTER 10   Lies About Hedge Funds and the Derivatives Market   185

CHAPTER 11   Lies About Government and Regulation   207

CHAPTER 12   The Real Reform Needed on Wall Street   221

INDEX   235

THE 86 BIGGEST LIES ON WALL STREET

1. Going into the current crisis, the American economy was the strongest and most resilient in the world.

2. This was simply a subprime mortgage problem that no one could have foreseen.

3. Government's insistence on lending to poor people who could not afford to buy a home created this problem.

4. The government, through its government-sponsored entities Fannie Mae and Freddie Mac, caused this crisis.

5. The problems were limited to the mortgage market.

6. This was a random event, like a hundred-year flood, that occurs naturally in the markets every fifty to one hundred years and could not be avoided.

7. Free-market capitalism works best with no regulation and no interference from government.

8. Corporations are just like people, only more rational.

9. Investment banks, commercial banks, rating agencies, and other middlemen are paid to represent your interests.

10. Capitalism works equally well in all industries.

11. If people were only more diversified in their investments this crisis would not have been as painful.

12. Lobbyists are good for the country and a great example of democracy in action: there are lobbies in Washington for grandmothers, pet owners, teachers, and all the rest of us.

13. The global banking system is adequately capitalized and will withstand this event.

14. Like the Great Depression, this is primarily a liquidity problem, and injecting cash into the system will solve it.

15. People are not investing and banks are not lending because they are afraid and are being irrational.

16. Taxpayer money is needed to bail out sick companies.

17. Everything that Hank Paulson ever said about the Troubled Asset Relief Program.

18. There are a few select large financial institutions that are the foundation of our banking system and, as such, are too big and important to fail.

19. We can save the auto industry with a $17 billion bailout by government.

20. Banks are more stable than investment banks because of their stable deposit base; therefore, it makes sense to turn investment banks, CIT, and GMAC into bank holding companies.

21. Diversification is the key. If everyone held a broadly diversified portfolio, the markets and society would be much more stable, efficient, and productive.

22. Buy low–sell high is a tried and true, guaranteed investment strategy.

23. The stock market will bounce back soon to pre-crisis levels, and so will the economy.

24. A buy-and-hold long-term investing strategy yields superior returns over trying to sell in down markets.

25. Dollar cost averaging, or buying in over time in small purchases, is a great way to achieve good returns without subjecting yourself to the risk of large losses.

26. Life-cycle investing means that people save during their productive years and then consume during their retirement years.

27. Technical analysis involving the charting of the historical prices of stocks can be very helpful in identifying buying opportunities or recognizing critical selling signals.

28. Before investing, you should talk with a financial advisor whose professionalism and long-term investing perspective will end up saving you a great deal of money over time.

29. In the long run, stocks outperform bonds if you do not object to slightly higher volatility along the way.

30. Stock market crashes are impossible today because markets are efficient; they properly and rationally price securities with all relevant information, making large one-day movements nearly impossible.

31. You should invest in companies with monopoly positions.

32. Annual cash flow (EBITDA) is a much more reliable measure of a company's earning potential than net income.

33. Companies selling addictive products, such as liquor and tobacco, make for good investments.

34. High inflation causes interest rates to peak and, because rates are higher, common stock P/E ratios become depressed.

35. The stock market's two-decade appreciation is primarily due to growth, innovation, the opening of new markets, and good management.

36. Low P/E stocks are considered bargains because they sell cheap relative to earnings, especially if they are big-dividend payers.

37. Fixed-coupon Treasury bonds are risk free.

38. Treasury Inflation-Protected Securities (TIPS) bonds are risk free because they adjust for inflation.

39. Interest rates are set by the Federal Reserve.

40. Bonds are a good investment and should represent a substantial portion of a typical individual investor's portfolio.

41. Tax-free municipal bonds are a good investment alternative for a tax-paying individual.

42. Private equity firms create value by taking a long-term perspective and growing the businesses they invest in.

43. Investing in stock options allows you a greater upside, with limited to no downside risk.

44. Venture capital funds are a great way of riding the high-tech wave.

45. Commodity prices are certain to drop further as demand evaporates in this global recession.

46. Ignoring current disruptions, housing is always a very good long-term investment.

47. Gold is a bad investment because it has few productive uses in industry.

48. Preferred shares are a better investment than common because they get paid first in bankruptcy.

49. Unemployment is currently 8.1 percent.

50. The current reported declines in real GDP are overstated.

51. Inflation is caused by an overheated economy with too little unemployment and greater wage demands by workers.

52. The Federal Reserve works for average Americans and is concerned with keeping the economy growing and vibrant.

53. Business cycles and recessions are necessary and normal to a well-functioning economy.

54. Big job growth in a country is an indication of a healthy, prosperous economy.

55. Tax cuts cause economic growth.

56. Greater country wealth, on average, brings greater happiness.

57. Social Security is a program that cares for our elderly poor.

58. GDP needs to keep growing for America's economy to be healthy.

59. Improved technology leads to increased productivity, which leads to a healthier and happier society.

60. Debt leverage is good because it increases shareholder equity returns.

61. CEO pay is deserved because it is determined in a highly competitive market.

62. The biggest advantage of the corporate form is to limit investor liability.

63. Complex financial instruments are tailored to benefit both the issuer and the investor.

64. The vast majority of mergers create enormous synergy value to the buyer.

65. Corporations pushed globalization to open new markets for their products.

66. Vast natural resource wealth is the best predictor of how wealthy a country's citizens are.

67. International trade has been proven to increase the wealth of nations.

68. Democratic reforms are bad for economic growth because the voting poor will organize and insist on income and wealth redistribution.

69. Capitalist countries enjoy greater prosperity, but pay for it with greater income inequality.

70. The US financial crisis and ensuing recession will be tempered and moderated to a great degree by the diversified global economy led by China and India.

71. The bigger our corporations and banks are, the better, as it makes them more efficient and stronger global competitors.

72. The European economic model of greater social support from government is a bankrupt ideology.

73. The credit default swap (CDS) market reduces risk in the system by allowing investors to hedge their exposure to default risk, and therefore has made this current crisis much more bearable.

74. The derivatives market should be unregulated to achieve maximum liquidity.

75. Individual companies benefit from the derivatives market because it smooths earnings and reduces volatility.

76. On average, hedge funds outperform the general market.

77. Investing in a fund of funds is a great way to minimize your risk if you want hedge fund–type returns.

78. Bernie Madoff found a surefire way to earn consistent, but not exorbitant, returns year in and year out.

79. Hedge funds should remain unregulated, because only sophisticated, knowledgeable investors can invest.

80. The current financial crisis was caused by too much government interference in the markets.

81. Government regulation is bad for economic growth and prosperity.

82. Rating agencies are regulated entities that work for investors to identify and price risk appropriately.

83. The SEC prevents insider trading and market manipulation.

84. Banks utilize off–balance sheet operations primarily to increase returns to their shareholders.

85. Chinese walls within commercial and investment banks prevent conflicts of interest.

86. Excessive regulation is not needed in the financial markets because anyone who is harmed can seek redress in the courts.

Introduction

I know what you are thinking. How was I able to narrow it down to just eighty-six lies?

The title of this book may sound funny, but I can assure you it is very serious. You see, it turns out that lying on Wall Street is not only painful to investors, but is one of the primary reasons why we are experiencing the current financial difficulties we face today.

The current economic crisis is not going to be fixed with tax cuts, increased government spending, more borrowing, or zero interest rates.

The cause of the current economic crisis is much more fundamental and structural in nature. Our entire financial system over the years has been corrupted.

By examining the biggest lies coming out of Wall Street we will begin to uncover how this corruption was allowed to occur and how endemic it is to our largest corporations, our biggest financial institutions and, yes, our government.

The first part of the book will focus most of its attention on an explanation of how the deception from Wall Street and the business community was able to translate into a broken financial system, stalled capital markets, a credit crisis, and an economy in freefall. We will explore the fundamental reasons for the current crisis, which will lead to a better understanding of a potential solution.

Much of the rest of the book is focused on making you a better and more knowledgeable investor and businessperson. While the issues discussed in the remainder of the book also contribute to the current problems we face today, I also present some very fundamental deceptions that Wall Street has long employed to bilk its investors and clients out of their hard-earned money.

It is the nature of the world today that all professionals have become much more skilled, but in more narrow areas of expertise. Some of our most brilliant minds become medical doctors and lawyers, but often so concentrate on medicine and law that they are exposed to very little sophisticated finance and investing techniques.

If they depend on their newspapers and television for their finance training they will be sorely disappointed. Journalists make poor finance professors. To begin with, they are excellent writers, so their left-brained mathematical skills may be somewhat lacking. Second, if they had a real interest in pursuing finance it would be much more profitable to do it at a Goldman Sachs than at the *New York Times*, at least until recently.

So this is my attempt to improve that imbalance. I have decades of financial and economic training and can speak firsthand about some of the tricks and deceptions I saw practiced upon unsuspecting clients on Wall Street.

Wall Street is littered with the lost fortunes of doctors, dentists and lawyers who knew just enough about investing and finance to think they knew it all. As they say, if you do not know yourself, Wall Street is an expensive place to find yourself.

What does the current financial crisis have to do with lying and corruption? Everything. Economies around the world are basically split into two camps: successful, highly developed countries with good growth prospects, and poorly run developing countries that stagnate at very low levels of output and incomes per capita.

A great amount of research has been accomplished trying to explain this dramatic split. I say dramatic because developed countries typically have annual incomes per capita of approximately $50,000 per person, while developing countries can have incomes per capita of just $1,000 to $2,000 per person. If you believe, as I believe, that people are fundamentally the same the world over, of pretty much equal average intelligence, such a dramatic difference in productivity is quite striking, and needs explaining.

It turns out that most of the developed world is both democratic and capitalist. Much of the poorer developing world is run by dictators, and while they are not entirely communist or socialist, they have very faulty economic systems.

The primary ingredient missing from the developing world that prevents economies from flourishing is good institutions. Different economists mean different things when they talk about good institutions. There must be institutions in place in a society that ensure the game called commerce is a fair game with just rules.

That is why most economists believe the rule of law to be one of the most important institutions in a successful economy. The rule of law encompasses the entire justice system, including our court systems, our judges, and our police, but also covers our legislative process and our ability to make rules, regulations, and laws that are fair and balanced for the electorate.

Why is fairness so important in an economic system? Simple. In an unfair system where one small group has a decidedly unjust advantage in getting ahead, other participants may choose not to play the game, not apply themselves in school, not work hard, and definitely not utilize their energies to innovate and be creative. If a great percentage of your population drops out of productive life because they do not see opportunities opening up for them within the system, you cannot have a broad-based, successful economy.

We can ask: where do these demands for fairness and justice come from? I do not believe they are in our genes, although it has been found that many mammals, such as dogs, get upset if they are fed bread as a reward in the laboratory while their fellow canine laboratory companions are rewarded with sausage. We may have an innate sense that fairness helps us get along better as groups and maybe this sense of equity is inbred in us, evolutionarily speaking.

But the great advances in humans demanding fairness and justice came in the Renaissance and the Enlightenment through knowledge and education. The shift of focus was from gods and kings to the individual and the sanctity of his or her ideas and his or her life. The great ideas of the period were built around ensuring that each individual could participate productively in a society that also guaranteed him or her the opportunities needed to live his or her own life free from interference by others. Eventually this discussion evolved into how people could form cooperative governments that protected individuals' rights to life, liberty, the pursuit of happiness, equal opportunity, fairness, and justice.

Yes, many of the poorest countries on earth are dictatorships, but what I believe is missing is their public's insistence on individual freedom. Many of these countries' populations have never been educated as to Renaissance thinking and the Enlightenment. Once people in a country are exposed to the ideas of the importance of the sanctity of the individual and shown that all power resides in the people, it is very difficult for that country to ever go back to dictatorship.

Order in liberal democratic societies is dependent not on a king or a dictator, but rather on a set of laws, rules and regulations. So, also, are economic systems. You could not have an economic marketplace, and you could never develop sophisticated capital markets, without significant rules and regulations. The protection of property rights, the honoring of contracts, protection against fraudulent behavior in business, consumer protections, and the elimination of monopoly rents are examples of regulations that are necessary to ensure the proper operation of a capitalist economy or a properly functioning market.

Many today have come to the wrong conclusion that all regulation is bad, and that the markets would function beautifully on their own. This makes no sense. It is the nature of markets—which you would know if you have ever played the game Monopoly—that companies trend toward getting bigger and bigger with greater concentrations of power, and it is up to government to ensure they do not exercise monopoly authority. You cannot have a properly functioning market that properly allocates resources in an efficient manner if there is a monopoly power.

Similarly, it is not very efficient to have a market economy in which fraud is allowed. It is possible, but a great deal of wasted time and effort will be expended by all participants because they will be constantly checking on their trading partners and potential investors who they would have to daily suspect of fraud. It is much better to enact rules against fraud and concentrate the policing powers in a central powerful body like the government. Under such a properly operating system, businesspeople and laymen can enter into commercial activities very quickly, sometimes over the Internet or telephone, without having to worry about fraud, knowing that if it ever occurred it would be actively prosecuted.

You might think this discussion has very little to do with the United States, and specifically Wall Street, but you would be wrong. These very fundamental tenets of how markets work efficiently and properly is what Wall Street failed to recognize and what caused this crisis. Since 1981, when Ronald Reagan became president, the country has moved toward greater and greater deregulation. I believe it was driven by the business community, which had undue influence in Washington because of their enormous campaign contributions and lobbying expenditures. But they were so successful in implementing their deregulation ideology and a laissez-faire approach to business that now, even without their direct involvement, most economists honestly believe that less regulation is always better for business.

If you understand the fundamental reasons why markets have to be regulated, that they cannot exist without rules, you will begin to understand how misplaced this entire recent wave of deregulation was. In the case of financial institutions on Wall Street, deregulation efforts went so far as to almost push the bounds of no regulation. When there is no regulation, ethical firms may indeed continue to do business properly, but it certainly opens the door for lawbreakers and miscreants to steal and lie and cheat and get away with it.

Of course lying and cheating and stealing and deregulation and breaking laws was not limited to Wall Street over the last thirty years. I could have written a book about lying and cheating and stealing in the pharmaceutical industry, and I doubt I would have had to materially reduce the number of lies presented in my book. But I focused on Wall Street because I do believe that the crumbling of our financial markets is the immediate cause of our current financial crisis. I understand that government was a co-conspirator by allowing such deregulation, and that our representatives in Washington violated their oaths of office by responding to the wishes of Wall Street and big business rather than the electorate. But it has gotten so bad with campaign contributions and lobbying that I no longer think of government as a separate entity, but rather a minor subsidiary of big business and Wall Street. Being a US senator may sound impressive to you, but I can tell you they get their marching orders from Wall Street and corporate America. Senators that sit on the Senate Banking Committee have numerous contributors, but their biggest are always the large financial institutions they are supposed to regulate. I hate to say it, but the Senate has lost most of its prestige lately and has really become a group of order takers. A senator might make half a million dollars a year from his public appearances and writings, but he is also taking orders from Wall Street titans and making hundreds of millions, if not billions, of dollars a year.

This book is a mix of small lies and big lies. Some of them truly are lies, in that the fabricator knew it was a falsehood in advance and used his energy to convince the dupe that he was telling the truth. Other falsehoods presented here are actually more myths than lies, because I do not think even the purveyors clearly understand how wrong their advocacy of such positions are, so they are not intentionally lying because even they do not know the truth. But the power and energy with which the purveyors continue to repeat these mistaken myths elevates them to such a level of seriousness that I wanted to include them in this book.

Some of the ideas that I discuss in this book are incredibly powerful ideas. It does not do them justice to bury them amidst eighty-five other fabrications and distortions.

For example, lie number 21 says that following a diversification strategy will minimize your risk and maximize your returns over time. I argue that this commonly held belief, taught to every business school graduate in the country, may indeed be wrong.

If I am right about the problems that result from investors pursuing complete diversification, it may fully explain how the current economic crisis became so huge and unruly. While it is but just one lie in this entire book, if I am right about diversification's shortcomings, it threatens all financial markets because diversification is the primary foundation underlying how all risks, assets and securities are priced in the market.

I never hesitate to present an idea I believe is right just because it sounds radical, dramatically different from the status quo, or hard to implement. Books are the place for ideas. When readers are exposed to powerful new ideas it leads them closer to supporting meaningful change and productive reforms that initially may have appeared too radical to consider.

So what exactly did go wrong in this current financial crisis? Many have labeled it a subprime mortgage crisis, but that is totally unfair; it started with subprime mortgages, but even these did not involve historically poor credit customers. Rather, the initial housing boom and bust was created by banks that were overly aggressive in the amount of money they lent to home buyers. Like all banks do, they first created a boom by over-lending, then they created a crash by restricting lending.

At the same time the banks were lending too much to home-owners, the banks were repackaging these mortgage securities, selling them upstream to long-term investors, and very quickly getting them off their books. Banks had no incentive to be certain that these mortgages would ever be repaid.

Long-term investors, like pension funds and sovereign governments, that ended up holding these mortgage securities were duped by investment banks, commercial banks, and especially the rating agencies into thinking they held AAA securities when they actually held the equivalent of securities trash.

But the story does not end with subprime mortgages. We shall see that even prime mortgages are experiencing dramatically increased default rates and foreclosures, and that the banks will realize significant losses in their prime residential mortgage portfolios. The greatest price increases in the country during the housing boom were in our wealthiest cities and neighborhoods, and thus they will have the biggest declines. Places like New York, San Francisco, Boston, Miami, Las Vegas, Phoenix, and San Diego are all going to see very significant declines in their home prices.

Most importantly, the story does not end with just mortgages. All commercial bank lending is going to get into trouble. First, it appears that international lending is problematic, because many countries of the world including Ireland, Spain, England, New Zealand, and Australia are themselves going through housing busts. Commercial real estate lending is just now beginning to fall apart; office vacancies exceed 15 to 20 percent in some markets, and malls might as well give away their store space rather than try to find lessees.

Loans to the private equity business, the hedge fund industry and leverage buyout shops have basically ceased, and commercial bank losses in these areas will be tremendous, as much of that activity has stopped altogether. Junk bond credit spreads have widened tremendously and many companies that were considered high quality credits are now considered junk. Much of the commercial banks' commercial paper activities and money market funds have had to be saved by the US government with federal guarantees.

As the economy weakens and unemployment increases, the consumer lending sector is going to evaporate. The banks will find enormous losses in their credit card portfolio, their auto loans, and their student loans, in addition to their mortgage portfolio.

It appears that almost all the types of loans the banks made are bad, and it's worse than that. They made too many of them. The banks increased their leverage of debt to equity from 10 to 1 to close to 25 to 1 over twenty-five years. Now they have lots of bad assets but a much smaller equity cushion. If only 3 or 4 percent of their assets get in trouble, these banks become technically insolvent.

What fundamental error did the banks make to get themselves in such a position? Part of the problem was that their managements never acted in their shareholders' best interests due to principal agency problems. But even their shareholders seemed motivated to achieve maximum leverage and to take on very risky business, attempting to maximize their stock prices. There was very little concern for managing downside risk. I do not know if people thought that business cycles had ended, and that we were to remain forever in prosperous good times, or if they just got overly greedy and lost track of good investment management skills.

I know one thing: these companies and banks and investment banks got very big. As companies get bigger they can squeeze out competition. There are some economies of scale, but they also become more unwieldy and difficult to manage. To think that a board of directors that meets once a quarter is going to have any understanding of what a company the size of Citigroup is doing every day around the world is ludicrous. If twelve members of a board of directors came to work every day for ten hours a day they could not possibly supervise all of Citigroup's operations around the world. Citigroup is composed of hundreds of different businesses in hundreds of different countries offering thousands of different securities and products to their customers. You could study it for one hundred years and you would not comprehend all that is Citigroup.

So I would argue that bigness breeds unwieldy organizations that become more political each day and less effective in protecting shareholders' capital, managing risk, and maximizing returns. Big companies realized this and took the unfortunate step of creating risk officers and risk management departments. Now department heads suddenly found that they no longer had to worry about risk, that the risk management department would take care of that. So they ran willy-nilly into very high risk situations that a centralized risk management officer could not possibly keep track of.

And the risk management departments were typically headed by very quantitative people who typically came from computer software backgrounds. Risk management software was utilized throughout the financial industry to supposedly point out and minimize risk. While computers may be able to beat humans in chess, they are not sophisticated enough to evaluate and rate risk in all of its different forms in literally millions of different markets for products and industries and businesses around the world.

I will give you a simple example. I was interviewed for a popular software and computer website by a journalist who was doing a study examining why these sophisticated risk management software programs were unable to uncover the potential crash in the housing market, while someone like me, armed with a single laptop computer, could successfully predict the crash and write two books about it in 2003 and 2006.

I asked him how many of the six risk management officers that he had interviewed at the major financial institutions had looked at the probability of house prices declining in the future after they had increased fifty years in a row. His answer: none. Risk management offices are supposed to be conducting "what if" scenarios and sensitivity testing to predict how a change in the current situation will impact the company's cash flow and earnings. And yet not one of these financial institutions' risk management officers attempted to answer the most basic question of all, What if house prices declined in the future?

Second, I asked this journalist how many of his six interviewees at the major financial institutions tried to predict what would happen to the foreclosure rate if housing prices declined. Again, he said none. To me, that was the key to the entire crisis. It was apparent to me, though not to most risk management software computer programs, that as house prices declined in value there would be a tremendous increase in the foreclosure and default rates. The reason is that if a homeowner gets in financial trouble during a boom in housing prices, he will not default on his mortgage and allow the bank to claim the valuable home; he will sell in the marketplace and use the proceeds to pay off debt and preserve his equity investment.

However, if a homeowner is in a declining home price environment, and is highly leveraged, it would make no sense to try to sell the property in the marketplace because it would be worth less than the mortgage amount. Rather, he would simply mail the keys to the bank. So, as housing prices began to decline, a simple computer analysis might have suggested that it would be helpful to increase the foreclosure rate by some 10 percent and see what that does to earnings. But based on the simple analysis I present here, I asked the question, What would happen if foreclosure rates increased 500 percent? It turns out I was right. The foreclosure rates have exploded in this country. I think it was easily predictable. The computers did not think so.

It is not all bad news. The great thing about finding out the cause of a crisis is that if you are right, the solutions become obvious. At the end of this book I will focus an entire chapter on the reforms that are necessary to straighten out our broken financial markets and our declining economy. They get at the basic structure of how we organize ourselves politically and economically as a society. It makes sense that the solution to the problem is radical and fundamental, given the severity of the crisis.

Following is a brief summary of the chapters presented in this book.

First, I present the lies and deceptions that I believe got us into this financial mess we call a crisis. In the first chapter I confront Wall Street's explanation of the current crisis as being caused by too much government interference. They like to point to Fannie Mae and Freddie Mac as causing this crisis, forgetting that Fannie Mae and Freddie Mac are not part of the government, but are actually private for-profit businesses and two of the biggest lobbyists in the world, and that Fannie Mae and Freddie did not issue any new subprime loans. I explain why long-lived industries like banking need regulation and have difficulty operating without it. I also explain that most lobbyists are not working on your behalf.

In the second chapter I examine in more detail the best way out of this financial crisis. I expose the lie that this has been caused primarily by a liquidity crisis. I attack those who say that people are being irrational and fearful, and that all we need is for people to become more confident in the markets. It is not right that bailouts are being executed with taxpayer money while creditors are getting out scot-free.

In the third chapter I try to refute the lies and myths surrounding proper investment strategy. I suggest that there would be a major problem if everyone followed a fully diversified approach to investing. I show that simple investment strategies like "buy-and-hold" or "buy low–sell high" may sound appealing, but are found wanting. And I expose technical charting analysis for what it is, complete rubbish.

In chapter 4, I attack stock investing lies. The biggest of these is that stocks outperform bonds in the long run. I then look at the performance of actively managed stock funds and the fees they charge, and whether it makes sense to invest in companies that have monopoly positions in their markets or in companies selling addictive products. I debate whether high inflation actually causes common stock P/E ratios to decline because interest rates head higher. I also challenge the assumption that high tech stocks necessarily deserve bigger P/E multiples because of their higher expected growth rates.

In chapter 5, I turn my critical eye to the bond market. I take exception to the most fundamental truths about bonds, namely that fixed coupon treasury bonds are risk free, that interest rates are set by the Federal Reserve, and that tax-free municipal bonds are a good investment for taxable individuals, or that bonds are a good investment in general.

I examine other investment markets in chapter 6. I try to fight people's misperceptions about private equity, venture capital, and hedge funds. I then examine commodity trading, gold trading, and whether it will ever make sense to invest in residential housing again.

Chapter 7 is an attempt to look at lies that have come out of the economics profession, such as the idea that business cycles and recessions are necessary and normal. There appears to me to be too much emphasis on growth in this country, and the idea that tax cuts can cause growth has never been proven. The simple statement that greater wealth brings greater happiness is also challenged.

In chapter 8, I do the same for the finance profession. I ask the question: what is the appropriate amount of leverage on a company? Also: is CEO pay deserved? I review whether mergers create value and why financial instruments become so complex.

In chapter 9, I take on the global economy and challenge the most basic of assumptions, that international trade creates country wealth. I show that vast natural resource wealth does not necessarily make a country wealthier. I ask whether corporations had other reasons to push for globalization in addition to opening markets for their products and services. I show that China and India are not of sufficient size to help end the current global recession.

In chapter 10, I try to correct misperceptions and falsehoods coming out of the hedge fund industry and the derivatives market. The derivatives market I am most concerned with is the credit default swap market and I expose it not as a method of hedging and minimizing risk, but one that dramatically increases systemic risk through speculation and through the interconnectedness it creates between companies. I examine whether hedge funds actually outperform the market and why funds of funds make little sense. I also explain why hedge funds and the derivatives market need to be tightly regulated.

I take on lies about the government and about regulation in general in chapter 11. Often it is suggested that industry can regulate itself, which I find laughable even though it is presented so seriously. I challenge the argument that all government regulation is bad for economic growth and prosperity. And I wonder whether it is true that free markets do best when left alone.

Finally, in chapter 12 I talk about the real reform needed on Wall Street. These needed reforms are extensive. They involve greater regulation, but I am also concerned that government is poorly suited to adequately regulate business. Currently, government itself is controlled by business, so any regulation they write will be fairly ineffective. Also, government has shown itself to be inept at managing almost any enterprise or regulation. Some academics have argued that greater regulation does not limit business, but is utilized by business to prevent competition in their industries and to secure and maintain monopoly positions.

Let us begin our trek through the wild world of Wall Street, where most everyone lies and where those that survive get very good at detecting deception.

CHAPTER I

Lies About What
Caused This Mess

Lie #1 Going into the current crisis, the American economy was the strongest and most resilient in the world.

This is one of the great lies that has been perpetrated on the American public for the last three or four decades. It is a central component of Wall Street's explanation of the current financial crisis, because Wall Street wants you to believe that everything was fine until a very limited problem called subprime mortgages exploded on the scene.

Nothing could be further from the truth. The American economy has been under great stress for a long time. While our GDP and the Dow Jones Industrial Average grew to record levels each year, this masked the real underlying underperformance of our economy.

GDP in America has been reported as growing for lots of reasons, many of which have nothing to do with improving the quality of life for the average American. First, GDP grew because the population increased. And much of the population growth was never fully reported, as it included millions of illegal aliens entering our country.

Second, United States GDP increased over the last ten to twelve years because borrowing increased during this time. Consumption by average citizens, big businesses, banks and our government all exploded, causing a dramatic increase in GDP, but much of this consumption and government spending was fueled by borrowing. The total amount of all debt outstanding in the United States has increased from $25 trillion to over $60 trillion in just the last ten years, and this does not include the unfunded liabilities in our Social Security and Medicare retirement and health care plans. Individuals have borrowed substantial amounts against their houses and used the proceeds to buy almost everything—automobiles, boats, vacations, etc. Similarly, governments have gone on a spending spree of their own. The US government has increased spending in the last eight years at the fastest rate in its history. It has seen an annual surplus in 2000 of $250 billion turn into a nearly $2 trillion deficit expected in 2009. And it has seen total government debt more than double from $5 trillion to $11 trillion. Something like $2 trillion has been spent on the wars in Afghanistan and Iraq, but this alone does not explain the huge increase in government spending.

Third, GDP has increased in the United States simply because many spouses have gone back to work. Not only does GDP increase by the wages of women who are newly working, it also increases because the working mother now has to pay for services she used to perform for free, such as babysitting, cooking meals, cleaning the house, etc. Those who stayed home always worked hard, but their efforts were not reflected in the GDP accounting. Now that they are, it appears that GDP has been growing rapidly, when in actuality all that has happened is that housewives have moved from being off–balance sheet to being on–balance sheet for GDP reporting purposes.

Fourth, there are many examples of things included in the GDP calculation that do not necessarily improve the quality of life for average Americans. Over $500 billion is spent each year trying to clean up pollution, which is both admirable and necessary, but we would not have the pollution if we had not had the GDP growth and industrial development that we have experienced historically. We did not measure the negative cost of pollution when we created it, but now we recognize as a positive contribution to GDP the cleaning up of that very same pollution. It does not make much sense.

Similarly, Americans spend close to a trillion dollars on defense and homeland security; we can debate how much more secure and safe we are from this spending, but one thing is certain: it cannot be economically productive to build bombs that destroy buildings and bridges and airports, and then pay construction companies to rebuild them. To the extent this circuitous logic ends up being reported as positive contributions in our GDP, it clearly overstates GDP.

So from a GDP perspective, America has not been doing as well as you would think. America has also been running a significant current account trade deficit each year. This means simply that we import much more than we export. Economists will tell you that this cannot continue forever, but it has continued for quite some time in America.

Inequality in America has been increasing over the last decade. Greater technology, lower union participation, and globalization have all caused a bifurcation in the earnings of Americans. Technology can spur high wage hikes, but it can also kill jobs in the low-wage, low-skill button-pushers category. Union representation in the private sector workplace has declined from a high of 35 percent in the late '50s to 9 percent today. Globalization has put working Americans in competition with one dollar per hour employees in low-wage China, Vietnam, and Mexico, while other Americans garnered the benefits of inexpensive imports and ownership in companies that utilized this low-wage labor.

Finally, as America goes, so goes the planet. The American free enterprise system has been successfully exported to many countries around the world over the last three decades. But it has not all gone smoothly. There have been a number of financial crises around the world: the Japanese real estate collapse in 1993, Mexico's peso crisis in 1994, the Asian flu economic crisis in Thailand in 1998, and Russia's default in 1999. Each of these crises was trying to tell us that not all was right with free-market capitalism as it was practiced around the world. Each of these warning signals was ignored until eventually the crisis hit home here in America on such a massive scale that it dragged all the countries of the world into a severe recession.

Lie #2 This was simply a subprime mortgage problem that no one could have foreseen.

It has been argued that the current financial crisis is simply a crisis in one narrow segment of the residential mortgage market called the subprime mortgage sector. This is just untrue. It is true that the crisis began in the subprime residential market for mortgages, but it certainly will not end there.

Most people believe that subprime lending means lending mortgage monies to people with bad credit histories. This is not necessarily so. People with poor credit histories were given more money than they should have been during this most recent housing boom, but you can also take a person with a fairly good credit history and turn him into a subprime borrower by extending him too much money on too generous of terms. Subprime only means that the borrower pays a higher rate, typically 3 percent more than a more conventional loan. He may do this because of a bad credit history, but he may also do it in order to minimize the down payment he put on the house, to increase the amount of monies he might borrow based on his reported income, to report no income at all on his application, or to avoid securing private mortgage insurance.

The reason subprime lending exploded first in this recession was that a great deal of it was being packaged and sold in the CDO market. CDO stands for collateralized debt obligations. Very simply, you can put a bunch of subprime poorly rated BB junk mortgage securities into a CDO, and because the lowest tranche of the CDO agrees to take the first hit if there are any defaults, the upper two-thirds to three-fourths of the CDO securities garner a AAA rating. It is the ultimate experiment in alchemy, to turn BB junk rated securities into AAA securities. And it is enormously profitable.

Many people believe that the fees taken out of the home buying process by mortgage brokers, bankers, appraisers and title search companies were exorbitant. They ain't seen nothing yet. When you take a $500,000 poorly rated subprime mortgage and turn it into an AAA rated CDO security, you have magically created more than $50,000 in value which you can quickly pay out for yourself in the form of fees and extra interest. The reason is that AAA securities do not have to yield as much to investors as subprime mortgages. Therefore a subprime mortgage that yields 8 to 9 percent can be repriced upwards such that its investor, who thinks he's buying a AAA security, will garner a lower yield typically associated with such high rated paper. The difference, which can be substantial, can be pocketed by the loan brokers and the bankers who sold the CDO.

Of course, this type of alchemy is all false. You cannot turn BB securities into AAA securities. And so, once the fraud was exposed to the investors, many of the CDO securities ended up trading at pennies on the dollar. This was the beginning of the banking and credit crisis.

But the housing and mortgage crisis is not constrained to just subprime mortgages. All home prices increased substantially in the United States during the housing boom, and it turns out that those in the wealthiest neighborhoods and the wealthiest cities increased the most. While subprime borrowers are going to be the first to default, they certainly will not be the last. You can see in regional maps of Los Angeles, San Francisco, or San Diego that the dramatic housing price declines of 35 to 40 percent occurred first in the less wealthy outer suburbs—Riverside in Los Angeles, Vista in San Diego, and Stockton in San Francisco. The wealthier neighborhoods did not decline as much. Most of the foreclosures that forced recognition of real price declines in houses occurred in the far outer suburbs of the cities, sometimes as far as sixty miles from downtown.

But prime borrowers in the wealthier neighborhoods of major American cities will end up seeing significant housing price declines and will see foreclosure rates increase. The reason is quite obvious. There is no way a wealthy resident on the coast of San Diego is going to continue to pay his mortgage of $2 million when the house across the street, very similar to his own, is on the market for $1 million. Even rich people will end up defaulting on their home mortgages. It is not that they will run out of money, it's just that they will refuse to continue to throw good money after bad.

This means that the housing crisis itself and the mortgage and credit crunch is far from over. It is just beginning to be felt in the wealthy enclaves of Los Angeles, Santa Monica, Santa Barbara, and even Manhattan. But it will be felt. The cause of the housing crash was the housing boom that preceded it, and the cause of that housing boom was too much money being extended by banks for home purchases primarily in the wealthier areas. While the country as a whole saw home prices nearly double over the last two decades, wealthier cities such as Las Vegas, Phoenix, San Francisco, Los Angeles, New York, Boston, and Miami saw real home prices appreciate from 300 to 600 percent. What goes up must come down.

Lie #3 Government's insistence on lending to poor people who could not afford to buy a home created this problem.

This is one of the funnier lies being told about the current crisis. If you remember, in the 1990s when the government's operating budget was in deficit and completely out of control, conservatives tried to blame the shortfall on welfare mothers. Blaming the poor is an age-old pastime. To suggest the poor have enough power in America today to cause any of our major problems is a joke. The power in America resides in her wealthiest families and her biggest corporations. The poor have nothing to do with the governing of the country.

During the most recent election, conservatives tried to blame ACORN and other community development groups that are counseling poor people to prevent them from being ripped off by predatory lenders. Without examining ACORN's historical default rate, these conservatives simply argued that ACORN had put poor people into homes they could not afford, causing the current crisis. How ACORN's total mortgage lending to all of its members of only $5 billion could have brought on a $30 trillion worldwide financial crisis was never explained.

The idea that poor people buying homes they could not afford was the cause of the crisis grew from a misunderstanding of what subprime lending was. Most of the problematic subprime lending occurred in Florida and California, and much of it was by middle- to upper-income families stretching to buy homes in the $400,000 to $1 million range. There is no way, even with fraudulent mortgage applications, that poor people could afford such homes.

Conservatives also are trying to blame the Community Reinvestment Act (CRA), again an attempt to make it appear as if Congress was pushing homes on poor people that they could not afford. The CRA says that banks, if they take deposits in a poor neighborhood, must also make loans in that neighborhood. Again, the biggest boom in housing prices over the last fifteen years was in our wealthiest cities. I can assure you that there were very few CRA mortgages extended in La Jolla, Beverly Hills, or Miami Beach.

Homeownership did increase during the last fifteen years. And it is true that many of these new homeowners ended up defaulting on their mortgages. But the number of new homeowners who defaulted were a small percentage of the total foreclosures in the country. No, the majority of defaults and foreclosures occurred with middle-class and upper-income Americans. Poor people, as always, were the first to be laid off and the first to be put under financial pressure, and as such were the first to default, but they certainly will not be the last.

Lie #4 The government, through its government-sponsored entities Fannie Mae and Freddie Mac, caused this crisis.

Many Wall Street types and other conservatives have tried to argue that the primary causes of this housing bust and mortgage crisis were the government-sponsored entities Fannie Mae and Freddie Mac. Even I exposed Fannie Mae and Freddie Mac as overleveraged and poorly-run institutions in my 2003 book, *The Coming Crash in the Housing Market.*

Fannie Mae and Freddie Mac have always been poorly-run businesses. But it is important to remember that they are not part of the government; they are privately owned and privately managed businesses. They are profit-driven, just like any other financial institution. And they motivate their executives, their management, and their employees the same way as any privately run business, through the use of bonuses and stock options.

While Fannie Mae's record was not perfect during this period, it was not the primary cause of the problem. Fannie Mae and Freddie Mac got in trouble with their regulators and had to sell assets, not acquire them, from 2003 to 2006, the period during which the worst housing price increases occurred. Fannie Mae and Freddie Mac were on the sidelines during the worst episodes of this crisis. It was private financial institutions securitizing subprime mortgages worldwide through CDOs that led to this crisis. Eventually Fannie Mae and Freddie Mac themselves bought some subprime loans in the secondary market, but they were not the primary issuer of them. As a matter of fact, by definition, when a mortgage loan qualified for Fannie Mae or Freddie Mac issuance, it was not subprime. This is because the majority of Fannie Mae and Freddie Mac packaged mortgages were guaranteed by them.

The mistake conservatives make in blaming Fannie Mae and Freddie Mac is that they believe the government, through its regulators, was instructing Fannie Mae and Freddie Mac to increase homeownership by lending to unqualified buyers. What they do not understand is that the government did not tell Fannie Mae and Freddie Mac anything. Fannie Mae and Freddie Mac were two of the largest lobbyists and campaign contributors to Congress in recent history—over $150 million in campaign contributions in the last ten years, and untold lobbying expenditures. Congress and OFHEO, the entity that was supposed to regulate Fannie Mae and Freddie Mac, took their marching orders from Fannie Mae and Freddie Mac, not the other way around. I believe the entire argument of increasing home ownership was nothing more than a guise to allow Fannie Mae and Freddie Mac to avoid any regulation. As private businesses, Fannie Mae and Freddie Mac paid their executives hundreds of millions of dollars and made sure that Congress passed no law to successfully regulate them. In this regard, Fannie Mae and Freddie Mac were no different than other giant private financial enterprises. To suggest somehow that government controlled them or that they were part of government ignores the recent history of Fannie Mae and Freddie Mac's substantial involvement in directing our government to do whatever they wished.

Lie #5 The problems were limited to the mortgage market.

Since this crisis began, many pro-business types on Wall Street have tried to argue at first that this was limited to subprime mortgages, and once that turned out to be proven false, that this was solely a mortgage market problem. This was an important argument to them because they did not want the entire capitalist system to have been found at fault, but rather limit the damage to simply mortgages, which, while a very large market, could be explained as a mistake in implementation rather than a fundamental flaw in capitalist ideology.

Unfortunately, this was not the case. It is true that the subprime market for mortgages exploded first and that Alt A and then prime mortgages got in trouble next. But to suggest that this was solely a mortgage problem ignores the true underlying reasons for the severity of the crisis.

First, banks have been allowed to increase their leverage dramatically worldwide. Typically banks could not leverage themselves with debt and deposits more than ten to twelve times their equity base. Through creative accounting and off–balance sheet manipulations many US banks exceeded twenty to twenty-five times their equity in debt and depositor leverage. It turns out the European banks exceeded thirty-five times their equity base.

Such leverage in the financial system insures that any small problem is magnified quickly into a crisis. The reason is that with 30 to 1 leverage, a bank only needs to have problems with 3.5 percent of its assets and its solvency is threatened. The banks, threatened with insolvency, pull back on all lending, causing not only a financial crisis but an all-out recession. Banks, unlike other corporations, do not have to pay higher interest rates to depositors as their leverage increases because the deposits are guaranteed by the US government, an issue that may need to be addressed in the future.

Leverage in the system was not limited just to the commercial banks. As we said earlier, our government increased its leverage from $5 trillion to $11 trillion during the Bush administration alone, and this ignores the $30 trillion plus liability of Medicare and Social Security. In addition, corporations saw their debts increase in the last ten years from some $7 trillion to over $13 trillion.

In addition to corporations and our government, the American consumer dramatically increased his leverage over the last ten years. Borrowing on credit cards increased more than 100 percent to $2 trillion, while mortgage lending also doubled from $6 trillion to $12 trillion. Mortgages were no longer used just to buy homes; now mortgages were used like ATMs to take money out of a home and spend it on cars, vacations, and even second homes.

The dramatic increase in debt leverage in borrowing meant that the system itself was much more volatile. Leverage increases volatility. Think about your own experiences. If you are earning $50,000 a year you can live comfortably, but if you are earning $50,000 a year and have a $1 million home mortgage things become much more volatile. A slight decline in earnings can impact your entire net equity.

The second problem with too much leverage in the system is that all these debts and borrowings eventually have to be paid back. If borrowing continues to increase during the boom years, then leverage exaggerates the magnitude of any decline or recession. As the recession takes hold, leverage declines and the loans must be repaid. So instead of borrowing greater amounts to consume more, consumption slows and the existing borrowings have to be repaid. Imagine the difference in economic growth of a country whose total borrowings increased from $25 trillion to $60 trillion over the last ten years, and that now must deleverage and watch its borrowings decline from $60 trillion to a more reasonable $30 trillion or $40 trillion. You do not have $30 trillion of increased consumption due to the new borrowing, and you do not have an additional $20 trillion of consumption as you repay debt. Defaulting on the debt is no answer, as this just shifts the burden to the banking system, which is already insolvent. If the United States were to lose $30 trillion of consumption over the next five to seven years, this would be disastrous. It suggests that the recession we are in will be very deep and long-lived, and that GDP will show real declines north of 5 percent per year for the foreseeable future.

We shall see that too much leverage in the system was not the only problem or major cause of this crisis. Later we will discuss the importance of transparency, fraudulent activity, the agency principal problem, corporate lobbying, excessive consumption and the lack of regulation, as well as companies and banks becoming too big and interconnected to fail. These are all major contributors to this financial crisis. But it was not just mortgages that caused this problem.

Lie #6 This was a random event, like a hundred-year flood, that occurs naturally in the markets every fifty to one hundred years and could not be avoided.

Alan Greenspan tried to argue that this financial crisis was completely unexpected, impossible to have predicted—a hundred-year flood, a purely random event. While Alan Greenspan was officially a government representative, he really spoke for the entire free market community that believed that markets should not be regulated. He was a major advocate and follower of Ayn Rand's philosophy that argued that regulation only got in the way of the individual spirit of human enterprise best exemplified in a completely free market. Remember, Ayn Rand was a novelist, and novels are fiction.

First of all, I am living proof that this crisis was predictable, since I predicted it in my housing books of 2003 and 2006. You can argue, as one reader tried to on Amazon.com, that I was just lucky in my predictions. But given their exact accuracy that would have to make me the luckiest man on the earth. I not only warned that housing prices would decline, I said their biggest declines would be in Florida and California and that the country would see 25 percent price declines while individual cities on the coast would see declines north of 55 percent. I explained that the mortgage market would enter a crisis, and that because the majority of banks' assets were held in real estate-related fields, the banks themselves would be threatened with insolvency. I predicted the complete demise of the private mortgage insurance market, which has now occurred. I suggested that Fannie Mae and Freddie Mac would never make it through the crisis. In my first housing book I suggested the problem would be national, which violated the age-old promise that all real estate is local, and in my second book I suggested the problem would be international, which has now proven true. Ironically, the reviewer on Amazon.com who originally called me lucky about my predictions logged back on after Fannie and Freddie went bankrupt and conceded that I had been right—but maintained that I was just continuing with my lucky streak

No, this was not a random event. This was not due to the general business cycle. It had a real cause, and that cause was fundamental and structural. Our government, our financial markets, our largest financial institutions, and our biggest corporations entered into a corrupt business enterprise to rip off the American consumer and taxpayer. The entire mortgage financing business and much of Wall Street itself was corrupted, and through their campaign donations and lobbying they were able to corrupt our government.

Real estate agents pushed people into ever larger homes they could not afford, appraisers provided appraisals that were disconnected from reality in order to make fees, and mortgage brokers falsely changed and fraudulently manipulated mortgage applications to ensure that deals got done. Commercial banks packaged junk securities and called them AAA with the paid assistance of the rating agencies who were part of the complete criminal conspiracy. The purchaser of the securities, the world's largest pension funds, government institutions, international banks, and sovereign debt funds may not have been corrupt, but they were certainly ignorant. They relied on a AAA rating knowing full well that the rating agency was being paid by the issuer, not the investor, and did little further credit analysis before investing.

This entire fraudulent scheme could never have occurred without the complicity of our government representatives. But they did not sell themselves cheaply. The largest contributors to the campaigns of our congressmen and presidents over the last fifteen years have been the National Association of Realtors, the Mortgage Bankers Association, the American Bankers Association (representing commercial banks), hedge funds, investment banks on Wall Street, and of course Fannie Mae and Freddie Mac. Our Congress was paid to stand down. They were paid not to enforce existing regulations, not to pass any new legislation, and to deregulate, to remove old regulation from the books to allow our financial institutions the ability to do whatever they wished. You may find it surprising that this resulted in losses to our financial institutions, but I will explain later in this book how this could have occurred. For now, realize that these very same financial institutions and their executives took out hundreds of billions of dollars in profits and management bonuses during the housing and mortgage boom, so they were willing to risk some losses to keep the game going.

No, this was not a random event, this was a pre-planned and direct attack on the American consumer and the American taxpayer. Americans are now losing their jobs, losing their homes, and putting their families under tremendous stress because of the actions of Wall Street, our largest financial institutions and our biggest corporations. The fact that they paid off our government representatives for their complicity should not shift the blame to government. This was free enterprise at its best. We will address in the next lie why completely unregulated free enterprise is such a bad idea.

Lie #7 Free-market capitalism works best with no regulation and no interference from government.

It has been drummed into us for the last thirty years, since Ronald Reagan took office, that capitalism and the free markets work best when they are completely unregulated. Free-market economists have viewed regulation as nothing more than interference in the operation of a perfectly unregulated free market. They view markets as some sort of divine entities that reach a magical equilibrium that benefits all, and they see any interference, especially from government, as distorting this harmonious picture.

True students of economics will understand that there can be no free markets without regulation. If you look at the countries of the world, those that are doing the best not only have a capitalist economy, but a strong rule of law and typically a democratic government. It is not just that free people admire democracy and free markets, it is that free markets are not sustainable without the rule of law. Laws, regulations, and rules are exactly what capitalism needs to survive. You could not have a market-based economy without a rule protecting property rights. Contracts need to be enforced. Fraudulent commercial activity needs to be prevented. These are all government functions that private business cannot perform on its own.

So it makes no sense to talk about a completely unregulated free market. It is an oxymoron. It is internally inconsistent and illogical. You cannot have a free marketplace without regulation.

Of course, some countries of the world, like Peru and India, have too much regulation. If regulation creates so many bureaucratic steps and fees that entrepreneurs are prevented from starting new businesses, than regulation can be deemed excessive and can hinder economic growth.

That is the opposite of what we currently have in the United States today. We have a free enterprise system that not only is unregulated, but one in which industry is writing its own regulations by controlling congressmen in Washington through its campaign donations and lobbying.

When the cigarette companies were forced under new regulation to limit the advertising and promotion of their deadly product, Philip Morris's own law firm ended up writing the legislation for Congress. Hedge funds on Wall Street are the largest contributors to Congress and today still remain unregulated and non-reporting. In 1999, banks paid Congress to repeal Glass-Steagall. In 2001, Congress was paid to not impose any regulations on derivatives. In 2004, commercial banks, another major contributor to Congress, were allowed to increase their financial leverage from ten times to over forty times their equity base.

We used to argue that what was good for GM was good for America. In the brave new world of globalization this is no longer true. GM sells automobiles to Americans, but it hires Mexicans and Indonesians to build them. Since the wages paid to workers by corporations is the single largest expense item on their income statements, big companies are not interested in figuring out how to improve the quality of life of average Americans. Rather, they want to figure out how to eliminate the minimum wage law, how to reduce the power of unions, and how to lower wages and benefits for the average American—all necessary for boosting profits if the company is not innovating and growing.

Lie #8 Corporations are just like people, only more rational.

Many economists argue that corporations act just like people and can be assumed to be rational players in a free market. As a matter of fact, corporations might act more rationally than humans, if you define the word rational like an economist. The reason is that the courts have found that corporations have only one objective, to maximize profits to their shareholders. They are not concerned with anything else, and many have dropped many of their charitable and community support activities as a result.

But in this latest financial crisis we saw major corporations acting any way but rational. They appeared to put their entire companies at risk just to make a quick profit. How can we explain this?

One explanation is that these corporations simply did not understand the risks they were taking. I find this hard to believe, because in 2003, with very little background in real estate, I uncovered a systemic risk in the housing and mortgage business that was large enough to bankrupt the entire system. It is hard for me to imagine that these very bright executives were so ignorant about the risks they were taking.

The reason corporations cannot be trusted to act as perfect rational economic players in a financial system is that corporations are not operating entities themselves, but rather are controlled by their shareholders and their managements. You would expect their shareholders to have the same profit-maximizing and risk-minimizing objectives as the corporation itself. We will see this is not necessarily the case later in this book when I examine the importance of relative performance of fund managers and show how diversification distorted shareholders' motivations.

The extent to which shareholders have had a difficult time getting their interests represented in corporate boardrooms across the world suggests that managements may have had an undue influence on the direction of corporations. One very major recommendation to come out in response to this crisis is that boards of directors should be given real power over managements and should be completely independent, representative of shareholders, and without ties to the existing management team.

The dichotomy between a company's management and its shareholders is a classic example of the principal agent problem. The shareholder is a principal who is risking his money in order to obtain profit, and the management is a paid employee who acts as his agent in order to operate the company, hopefully to maximize those profits. One has to be very careful in how one structures management and employee compensation in order to ensure that their motivations align properly with those of the shareholders.

If management is solely compensated through a fixed salary, they will have no incentive to take risk or to increase profits for the business going forward. If one institutes a cash bonus system for management, there is the risk of its being misused to pay big bonuses regardless of true performance. Stock options as a motivational tool were given to managements in an attempt to better align their motivations with that of the shareholders, i.e., to tie bonus increases to the price of a stock over time.

But stock options themselves have real problems as a motivational tool. Employees given stock options have no investment in the company, so they do not care if it fails. This leads them to make excessively risky bets that, if right, dramatically increase the value of their stock options. If they are wrong, they simply walk away with no loss, leaving the shareholders holding the bag.

Managements in the future should be compensated with restricted stock rather than with stock options, and managements should be asked to pay a significant downpayment on any stock grants so that they have real skin in the game and can suffer losses just like shareholders if the stock price declines.

The concept of bonus pools by department should probably be eliminated, as it makes no sense to reward management and employees in a particular department while the entire company is either losing money or going bankrupt. Departmental performance can determine the amount of awards each year, but the award should come in the form of partially paid-for stock grants, not cash. Managements that take a percentage of profits out each year in the form of cash bonuses have a much shorter-term horizon than shareholders whose stock price depends on the long-time survival and long-term performance of the company.

Lie #9 Investment banks, commercial banks, rating agencies, and other middlemen are paid to represent your interests.

Part of the dilemma that individual American investors face in this crisis is that no one is on their side. While traditionally they have hired stockbrokers, financial advisors, investment consultants, mortgage brokers and real estate agents to provide them with expert advice, it is becoming increasingly clear that none of these individuals have their clients' best interests at heart.

We used to live in a simpler world where your agent got paid a fee and did well if you did well financially. The world is no longer that simple.

Consider real estate agents who only get paid if their client ends up buying a home. Given that there are numerous parties looking at the purchase of a home, this means that only one real estate agent, that of the winning buyer, will be paid. This suggests that the buyer's real estate agent is motivated not to get the best possible deal for the buyer, but to convince him to pay more than he wants to—in many cases, more than the home is worth. This is how the buyer's real estate agent gets paid: by representing the winning party and having his client overpay.

Things are not that much different on Wall Street. It used to be that investment bankers represented very large corporations, working as their agents to issue new stock, sell bonds, or buy or sell companies. This is also no longer true. The majority of profits on Wall Street today come from the trading business, and the majority of those profits come from principal businesses where the investment bank is no longer acting as someone's agent, but is taking positions in assets and securities for their own account.

This is a dramatic change. Now, if an investment bank comes to you, even if you are one of its largest corporate or investing clients, and offers you stock in a company for sale, it no longer means that the investment bank thinks it is a profitable investment. Rather, the investment bank may be on the opposite side of this transaction, and one of their principal investment arms or their trading desk is trying to unload this asset. When the investment banks decided to get into the principal business, they could no longer be effective agents for corporations and investors. They would not only keep the best investments for themselves, but would try to palm off on others those investment schemes that had not worked out.

In some ways, this has always been the case on Wall Street. Even before principal investing took off, there was a small naturally-occurring principal component to the agency investment banking business. A typical trade of stock on Wall Street would have a seller of 200,000 common shares and a buyer of 100,000 shares, and the Wall Street firm itself would have to position the extra 100,000 shares on its trading desk. The next day would begin with a morning conference call to all of its brokers worldwide pushing these hundred thousand shares on to the investment bank's clients. In essence they were unloading an unwanted asset. Of course they disguised the sale by getting their research department and their brokers to talk about the quality of making such an investment, but the real reason behind them pushing it was they were trying to unload it from their own balance sheet.

The rating agencies have historically been small middlemen in most transactions. What the big investment and commercial banks found out is that by paying them $10 million in fees instead of $200,000 on big issues, they could sway the thinking of the rating agencies and get them to be more generous in their assigned ratings. Once the rating agencies got in the business of calling BB junk securities AAA securities, their profits exploded. Their earned fees from the investment banks and commercial banks increased to billions of dollars where previously they'd been making tens of millions of dollars. Of course, their independent judgment was co-opted. It is surprising that none of their investment clients ever realized until it was too late that these rating agencies had been bought off by the issuers.

Many people today get their investment advice from television. There are a number of highly successful television programs that attempt to provide investment advice to their audiences. But do these audiences realize that these television programs' very existence depends on commercial advertising and keeping those commercial advertisers happy? In addition, these television programs themselves are owned by for-profit corporations. It is unlikely that an advertising-supported television program is going to be overly bearish on the stock market in general and certainly is not going to expose a major corporate problem like excessive government lobbying. I can speak from experience; whenever I have appeared on these programs and the subject of corporate lobbying comes up, there is an immediate change in the topic of conversation.

We'll see in a later chapter that middlemen in the investment process, like mutual fund advisers, may also not be trustworthy. They may be more interested in comparative performance relative to their peers than earning you absolute dollars. Their relative performance guarantees their success in raising money in the future, but it has little to do with your financial investing performance.

I believe we live in a new world where middlemen are not to be trusted. If this is true, it impacts how each of us manages our finances and invests our assets. We will address this in the coming chapters on investment alternatives.

Lie #10 Capitalism works equally well in all industries.

Capitalism's supporters would like it to be the case that capitalism is equally effective in all industries since it encourages individuals and corporations to maximize profits and thereby the well-being of society.

Ironically, now that the financial markets have collapsed, it might be performing a disservice to suggest that all of capitalism is broken.

Critics of capitalism have utilized the recent financial crisis to suggest that all of capitalism is a failure and that major changes must be made to all industries or that capitalism itself might have to die.

If we can show, however, that the financial markets and Wall Street are unique in some way, different from other industries, and that Wall Street is an example of how purely unregulated capitalism does not work well in the banking system, then we may be able to save other industries from abandoning a successful capitalist approach.

The banking system is unique in one regard. It deals with very long-lived assets and liabilities. These assets, like homes and businesses, can survive a hundred years, and their mortgages can certainly last thirty and forty years. This is far beyond the life expectancy of many senior managements at these banking institutions, and it certainly extends beyond their working years.

This means that managements at these institutions can do some fairly stupid things that will impact profits negatively over a long-term horizon, but that might generate additional cash flow in the short term. For example, a bank executive could push his institution into highly profitable subprime mortgages knowing full well that the defaults on such mortgages will not occur for years in the future, long after he is gone.

Capitalism, of course, does not guarantee that there will not be individual instances of bad management in the market. But the concept of free-market capitalism is that such bad players will be punished by the marketplace, and that their firms will not profit.

The problem with long-lived asset industries like banking is that the punishment is too long in coming. Consider this example: you own a donut shop in the middle of town and a new competitor opens up across the street, selling donuts for what everyone knows is half the cost of actually making them. The bad news is they will get 100 percent of the customers in town; the good news is they will very quickly go bankrupt, since selling products below cost is not a very profitable long-run enterprise strategy. Your short-term profits might suffer, but you will not feel pressure to match their silly pricing as you know they will very quickly succumb to the pressures of the market and go bankrupt.

Now suppose you run a mortgage bank in town and a newcomer opens a mortgage bank across the street offering no money down on very low interest, negative amortization, forty-year mortgage loans. Again, the bad news is that you will lose market share and customers. The further bad news is this new mortgage banker will not immediately go out of business. It will be years and maybe decades before his mispricing of risk shows up in actual defaults and foreclosures and ends up bankrupting his business. In the meantime, he will either garner 100 percent market share or you will be forced to match his pricing. This is what happened with the mortgage crisis in America. Because of the long-lived nature of the banking business, some aggressive and unscrupulous bankers began to misprice risk and offer terms that in the long-run were not profitable, but in the short run turned out to be enormously so. The sad fact is that well-meaning and well-managed banking operations had to match their stupid pricing terms or face extinction themselves.

Banking is not the only long-lived asset and liability business in the world for which capitalism does not work perfectly well. The insurance business has long been recognized as a very long-lived liability industry in which companies taking in positive cash flow in premiums have to maintain sufficient capital in the long run to honor their insurance contracts, and that is why the insurance industry is so highly regulated. There is no way, short of regulation, that the marketplace can prevent an unscrupulous competitor from dominating the insurance business by offering lower premiums with no intention of ever making contractually obligated insurance payoffs. It is the reason why all long-lived asset and liability industries must be regulated.

And this is the key. If the banking industry or the donut industry were a simple stand-alone segment of our entire GDP, it would be one thing. But the truth is that the banking system is the fundamental credit system for all of our industries. We are in a difficult position where the key component to our entire financial and economic health is our banking system, and yet we are now realizing that it must be regulated since it does not perform well under completely unregulated capitalist terms.

The solution is self-apparent. Many shorter-lived asset and liability industries like donut shops can be allowed to go fairly unregulated, letting competition to do its level best to maximize profitability for the industry as a whole. But banking and other long-lived asset liability industries must be regulated, and if we do not regulate them, we will force our economy, including all other industries, into violent boom and bust recessions and depressions as the banking industry itself tries to deal and cope with the unregulated nature of its existence. The choice is simple. Deregulate banks and force the world to suffer. Properly regulate banks with regard to their leverage and the riskiness of the businesses they enter, and you will eliminate the driving cause of most recessions and depressions.

Lie #11 If people were only more diversified in their investments this crisis would not have been as painful.

We will cover diversification in more detail in our investment chapter, but I wanted to mention it here because I believe it is a very important component to the current financial crisis, yet no one to date has mentioned it.

We have argued that the banking system was not properly regulated and that capitalist free markets themselves have trouble operating without proper rules and regulation. But a true free-market economist might take exception to this. What most surprised Alan Greenspan and other purely free-market advocates was that the system driven by profit motivation of each of its participants completely fell apart.

My ninety-two-year-old mother grew up in Kentucky in the small town of Lawrenceburg very close to the center of the most successful horse-breeding farms in the world. As a youth, she often showed horses for owners interested in selling them. She was the first to explain to me that the horse business was a completely laissez-faire operation. There was no regulation, and there was no such thing as fraud. If you could sell a twelve-year-old nag to someone looking for a three-year-old to run in this year's Kentucky Derby, all the better for you. Thus the expression, do not look a gift horse in the mouth; by examining the horse's teeth you can determine his age and hopefully avoid being taken in a sale. There is no government agency that looks at horses' teeth for you, and if you get taken in a horse trade, I can assure you, you will not have your day in court, at least not in Kentucky. That is why they call it horse trading.

So while being completely unregulated to the point of not even protecting participants against fraudulent lies and corruption, the horse business thrives. One cannot say whether it would do even better with appropriate commercial rules, but the lack of rules has not hastened its extinction. All participants know that they will have to make their own judgments as to the quality of horses they buy. Today, China has very little regulation with regard to its industry, and it has prospered. Free-market advocates are asking the same question about the financial crisis. Why could not the financial industry survive this latest crisis without regulation?

Without regulation in the financial industry each participant would solely be motivated by profits, and as such, his own self-interest. But according to Adam Smith, there is nothing wrong with greed; by acting selfishly the entire country benefits. Under such a system you cannot blame the real estate agents for giving bad advice to buyers in order to earn greater fees, and I do not think you can blame buyers for overpaying. Primarily, they were not spending their own money. Most were 100 percent financed by banks, so they were spending other people's money knowing full well that if somehow houses went down in price they could always walk away from the house and default on their mortgage. The appraisers, mortgage brokers, real estate agents and even the home buyers themselves under this scheme appeared to be rational, by economic standards. Under a laissez-faire unregulated market scheme, none of them appeared to be in a position of ever getting hurt if there was a housing downturn.

Next in line are the commercial bankers, who it turns out were not keeping these mortgage assets on their balance sheet, but rather packaging them in securitization schemes and selling them upstream. Because they were taking enormous fees upfront, garnering enormous profits by turning BB securities into AAA securities, and not positioning the assets, these commercial banks also cannot be claimed to be irrational in an economic sense. Selling their clients fairly worthless securities may have been unethical, but as we remember from our horse example, in a completely free unregulated market, ethics has little to do with economics. The rating agencies themselves did nothing wrong from an economic perspective by inflating their ratings unjustly; they were just maximizing their fees. Again, completely unethical, but profitable.

The real loser in this entire mortgage financing business was the end buyer of the mortgage securities. These included the pension funds, the sovereign governments and their commercial banks, the insurance companies, and other investors that ended up holding these fairly worthless mortgage securities. One explanation is that these investors were simply lazy and depended too much on the rating agencies to guarantee they would not face losses. This seems overly simplistic today.

I think the fundamental reason why this global laissez-faire system failed is that it depended too much on diversification. Diversification has been preached at all of our leading business schools for decades as the key to minimizing risk and maximizing return. But to accomplish the ultimate in diversification it means that commercial banks in Germany have to hold some percentage of their assets in US mortgages. To me this makes little sense. Commercial banks in Germany know very little about the commercial and residential real estate markets in the United States. They either have to depend on middlemen to assess that risk for them—and we have said earlier that many middlemen are not to be trusted— or they must trust that the efficient market itself will properly price all risk, making it unnecessary for them to worry about overpaying.

You see, that is the beauty of the theory of efficient markets. All assets are properly priced relative to risk, because if they are not, arbitrageurs would step in and correct the price. If you believe this efficient market theory, this means you yourself do not have to do any investment analysis research or investigation of managements and their companies. You can rely on the market to properly price all assets. It is very similar to betting on a horse at a track without doing any analysis; you will probably get the right odds because many others have done the analysis and properly assigned the right odds to the horse.

I think this is the mistake that these very large institutional investors made with regard to mortgages and other assets and with regard to the pricing of risk. They assumed that by being properly diversified they would minimize their risk, but their diversification strategy itself required that they hold so many assets that they did not have the time to evaluate risk and return for each. Rather, they allowed the market to properly price the assets for them.

In such a passive, highly diversified world, in which few are doing fundamental investment analysis, it almost ensures that the market itself will become corrupted. If no one is watching the store, someone will come in and rob you blind. I think private equity firms and hedge fund firms made a living off of the passive investment philosophy adopted by very large institutional investors around the world. The investors had been lulled to sleep by the false promise of diversification and efficiently and properly priced markets.

Lie #12 Lobbyists are good for the country and a great example of democracy in action: there are lobbies in Washington for grand-mothers, pet owners, teachers, and all the rest of us.

Recently, I have seen a number of news reports from reputable organizations like CNN, the *New York Times* and the *Wall Street Journal* suggesting that it is unfair of us to attack lobbyists. Their basic premise is that lobbying is good. They then go on to argue that lobbyists represent all of us. They say there are lobbyists for our grandparents, for our pets, for everyone.

Such blatant lies make me honestly concerned about the inde-pendence of our media. Much of our media is corporate-owned, and as such there are few reports about the damaging influence of corporate lobbying. But to come out with reports of blatant support for the practice of lobbying is scary.

It is true that our pets have lobbyists in Washington. But the spending that those pet lobbyists do is dwarfed many thousands of times by the amount of money spent by corporate lobbyists. Lob-byists and campaign contributors fall into two broad categories. The first is corporate lobbyists who lobby on behalf of our biggest corporations, banks, hedge funds, and financial institutions. The second is composed of organizational lobbyists that lobby on behalf of groups of Americans, whether they be environmentalists, the elderly, union members, or teachers.

While I believe all lobbyists do great harm to democracy because they prevent broad participation in decisions that affect us all, there is no question that corporate lobbyists do the most harm. At least, when lobbyists interfere with the democratic process on behalf of large organizations of people, they are representing Americans, albeit not necessarily all Americans. When they lobby on behalf of corporations, they are representing no one but the corporation and its shareholders. It violates economic theory for any corporation to be so sufficiently large and powerful as to itself influence the marketplace, and it is an unfathomable violation that a corporation participating in an economic marketplace would also be influencing the rulemaking of that marketplace.

Regardless of what the Supreme Court says, corporations are not persons. They should not have the rights of persons. We should be able to investigate them and demand full disclosure from them, and journalists should have access to their inner workings to assure they are not dependent on fraud and corrupt activities for their profits. They should have no right of secrecy. And a corporation certainly should not be able to petition the government or lobby. Laws are written to protect the American people, not corporations. When corporations get involved in writing legislation they do not have the people's interests at heart, only their profits. As such they want to make sure that they can pollute the environment, refuse to implement any global warming initiatives, damage union membership and hold down workers wages, prevent government from monitoring the workplace and its safety, and prevent government from properly regulating the quality of products, including the quality of food and drugs.

It really is not true that our government is not effective. It has been very effective in passing legislation favorable to the corporations who have been paying it. It has facilitated globalization while it has done nothing about global warming, to the great glee of corporate America; it has enforced intellectual property rights and patents for new products and new drugs around the world; it has lengthened copyright and patent protection periods; and it has created loopholes such that very few large corporations pay any corporate income tax at all.

No, it is not that our government is ineffective, it just reports to a different boss than the American people. While Congress has done a very good job delivering on the wish list of corporate lobbyists, it has done almost nothing to aid the American public. Problems important to the American public like low wages, unemployment, a weakening education system, overly expensive health care and pharmaceuticals, and a planet slowly rising in temperature have not been addressed by Congress because their allegiance has been to corporations and their lobbyists.

CHAPTER 2

Lies About How to
End the Crisis

Lie #13 The global banking system is adequately capitalized and will withstand this event.

Not to scare you, but the entire global financial system is bankrupt. Not a single investment bank or commercial bank in the world would be solvent today if all of their liabilities were recognized, including guarantees and insurance they have provided, and if all of their assets were properly marked to market.

This is an incredible statement. If 10 percent of the world's banks were insolvent, we would be in crisis. I am suggesting all of them are insolvent.

Subprime mortgages, where this crisis began, were sufficient by themselves to drive many of our largest financial institutions into bankruptcy. Those that remain publicly traded ongoing entities are themselves insolvent even though they have refused to admit it. They over-inflate the value of their assets and understate their liabilities in order to mask how serious a problem they face. If any bank disagrees and believes they are still solvent, I offer them this challenge. Let me inside the tent to examine your books for a week. That should settle it. I doubt I will get any takers on my offer.

But as we said before, the subprime mortgages only represented $1.3 trillion in assets in a $50 trillion problem. Commercial banks in the future will face much greater losses on their prime mortgage portfolios as defaults and foreclosures spread into the wealthier neighborhoods where the greatest increase in home prices occurred and which are most susceptible to dramatic house price declines.

All lending at commercial banks is threatened. Half of the hedge funds in the world will fold up shop as a result of this crisis and the sharp decline in the value of stock markets around the world, as well as the decline in the value of corporate and municipal bonds. Hedge funds are very big borrowers from the commercial banks.

Not just residential home lending, but commercial lending is facing very tough times at the banks. Vacancy rates in office buildings are increasing dramatically, apartment rent rates are dropping, and malls have been all but vacated. Banks are getting stuck with half-completed projects as construction loans are pulled.

Banks' corporate lending is way down and defaults are sure to increase as more and more corporations claim bankruptcy, leaving banks out in the cold in trying to collect commercial paper and investment grade corporate debt, as well as junk-bond credits. The entire business of leveraged buyouts and private equity investments has ceased, and with it an enormous loss to the banks in the form of corporate bridge loans and senior corporate debt to highly-leveraged companies.

But the consumer portfolio at our commercial banks is in no better shape. We know about the losses to date in their mortgage portfolios, but their losses in credit card lending, student loan lending, and auto loans is just now beginning to increase. Much of this lending landed on a securitization market that has all but ceased to exist. As personal bankruptcies increase, defaults on student loans, car loans and credit cards will increase dramatically.

Basically, the entire revenue side of the commercial banks business has disappeared. But the banks cannot adequately decrease their exposure to expenses by a proportional amount. Investments in people, real estate, buildings, and business systems do not allow a commensurate decrease in expenses as revenues decline. Because the banks are so highly leveraged, bad loans across all sectors of the business will threaten all of them. Given what is happening in all of these bank lending markets, there is no way banks capitalized with 3 to 5 percent equity could possibly survive.

There are some smaller regional banks who to date have avoided the subprime problem and the mortgage problem by selling almost all of their mortgages upstream to money center banks. They will not be so lucky in the coming recession. As job losses multiply they will experience far greater default rates on their consumer loans, and as businesses bankrupt themselves, their commercial real estate lending and business lending will suffer great losses.

When commercial banks lie about their current condition, they prevent implementing a quick and effective solution to the current crisis. Until we address the asset quality of our banks and their threatened insolvency we will never recover from this crisis. Japan had a similar experience with bad real estate losses at their banks in 1993, and by not addressing the solvency question of their banks, they ended up delaying recovery for more than a decade.

If you are going to waste trillions of dollars trying to accelerate a recovery from this crisis you ought to spend it where it can do the most good. That is to put our financial institutions on a firmer foundation. Rather than bailing out the weakest members of the group, there should be an accelerated bankruptcy procedure in which banks' managements can be replaced, banks' creditors can take a financial hit, and with the help of government funding our banking system can be properly capitalized to provide credit for a growing and recovering economy.

Lie #14 Like the Great Depression, this is primarily a liquidity problem, and injecting cash into the system will solve it.

Ben Bernanke, the chairman of the Federal Reserve, is a great student of the Great Depression. Most economists, including Bernanke, believe that the Great Depression was exacerbated by the Fed tightening the money supply during a difficult economic period. It is true that the money supply declined during the early years of the Depression, but this was primarily due to the large number of banks that claimed bankruptcy, reducing the deposit base of the country and thus reducing the money supply.

Just because the money supply declined during the Great Depression as the economy slowed does not mean the money supply contraction caused the recession to be worse. In fact, as explained above, the Depression caused the money supply decline. It is accepted wisdom among economists that money supply contraction and resulting deflation is bad for economic growth. This is not necessarily true. There is no reason why an economy cannot do very well with a reduced money supply and the decreasing nominal prices. Look at the computer industry. Prices of electronic chips and laptop computers decline every year and yet this does not prevent companies like Apple and Microsoft and Cisco from doing very well.

So the presumption of almost all economists is that loose money causes economies to grow. Certainly, loose money causes normal prices to increase, but there is no proof that such a policy results in real economic growth.

Because of his academic research on the Great Depression, Bernanke's answer to the current crisis is that it is a liquidity problem that can be solved by injecting more money into the system. Even if the Great Depression was made worse by tight money, this does not mean the current crisis is similar or has anything to do with a liquidity problem.

In fact, the current crisis is not a liquidity problem. Bernanke and Paulson have tried numerous times to inject literally hundreds of billions, if not trillions, of dollars into the system with almost no effect on loosening up the credit extended by banks. The reason is simple. It is not a liquidity crisis; it is a bank solvency crisis.

Banks are not lending, but the reason is not because they have no money and no liquidity. It is because they are nearly insolvent. They have so many bad loans on their books that their entire equity base is threatened with the risk of bankruptcy. The last thing they want to do is enter into more risky loans that may further threaten their solvency.

The ultimate proof that this is not a liquidity problem is that the banks are now sitting on close to $1 trillion in reserves. As they are given more and more money by the Fed they do not lend it, they just sit on it. Even those banks that were literally given hundreds of billions of dollars by the Treasury and Hank Paulson through his TARP plan are not relending it. Some have made acquisitions, but most are just reinforcing their equity base, which is what you would expect companies to do whose equity bases are threatened with bankruptcy. Eugene Fama has written an article that argues that the equity infusions to the banks did nothing helpful; it was a direct wealth transfer from the taxpayer to the banks' creditors, who certainly appreciated the greater capital cushion below them.

The risk of injecting trillions of dollars worldwide into the global financial system is twofold. One, if the monies are borrowed by the governments of the world, they eventually will reach their debt capacity and be unable to fund other more meaningful, and hopefully more effective, means of ending the recession. Second, if they print new money to fund this monetary expansion, they risk turning inflation loose in a declining economic environment—the definition of stagflation, high unemployment and high inflation. In an ironic twist, general inflation would reduce debt loads and probably help the economy in the short run.

The bottom line is that everything that Ben Bernanke and Hank

Paulson did, involving putting trillions of dollars toward trying to increase liquidity, has had almost no effect on reducing the severity of the recession. The reason is that the recession is not being caused by a liquidity crisis, but by a bank solvency crisis, and the reason the banks are insolvent is because of much more fundamental problems in our financial system, our economy, and how our government regulates the two.

Lie #15 People are not investing and banks are not lending because they are afraid and are being irrational.

I often hear that the primary problem causing the current economic downturn is that people and investors have been overcome with fear. The presumption is that people are acting irrationally based on this emotional response of fear and if they would only act more rationally they would see the great bargains that exist in stocks today and banks would realize all the good lending opportunities available in the marketplace.

This is hogwash. Banks and investors are acting completely rationally given the current market circumstances. First of all, I cannot think of any scenario in which the economy is going to do much better in the short term. I can tell many stories of how the Dow Jones may end up at 5,000, but I cannot think of any story where it returns to 14,000 in the foreseeable future.

The reason banks are not lending and investors are not investing is because there is no transparency. Everyone knows that many of the banks have bad loan problems that they are not disclosing along with the financial risks they bear in the derivatives market. Similarly, everyone is concerned that many of our largest corporations have not fully disclosed their operating problems.

The reason the interbank lending rate got so high is not because banks are afraid and irrational, it is because they do not know where the bad assets are in the system. They do not know who is at most risk of bankruptcy so they do not want to lend to other banks. Like me, if they are smart, they probably realize that almost all the financial institutions in the world are technically insolvent. It would be irrational to continue to lend to these institutions in such an environment.

The solution is not to insist that banks lend money or to give them more liquid funds. The solution is to insist on strict transparency of all lenders, and more: every company in the world should be forced to report in detail all of its assets marked to market, all of its liabilities, and any guarantees it has made, including those in the credit default swap market. This reporting could easily happen on the Internet in such detail that all the credit quality problems in the world would be universally exposed.

Of course, this begs the bigger question, what to do with the truly insolvent firms that result from such a transparent exposure. The answer is that we must accelerate our bankruptcy proceedings so that they take weeks rather than years. Truly insolvent companies, especially banks, need to reorganize quickly, eliminate ineffective managements, haircut their debt investors and creditors, and reemerge as newly solvent and ongoing enterprises immediately.

This has all happened once before. In 1993, Japan's banks, which had been over-lending for decades, suffered enormous losses in the Japanese real estate and stock market. Rather than immediately restructuring and admitting their problems, the banks hid their problems for years, causing Japan to go into a recession that has lasted more than a decade. Again, the banking industry is critical to a successful economy, and if you let it suffer for years your economy will suffer along with it for decades.

We can take the tough action that is required to straighten out the banking industry now or in ten years. The difference is that we will have missed an entire decade of growth if we delay.

Lie # 16 Taxpayer money is needed to bail out sick companies.

Every single company bailout that the government has made to date has involved the utilization of taxpayer monies. J.P. Morgan would not buy Bear Stearns without the government guaranteeing $29 billion of bad assets. Fannie Mae and Freddie Mac were taken over when the government injected $200 billion (now $400 billion) in a preferred stock issue, but the total cost to taxpayers will end up being multiples of that. Morgan Stanley, Goldman Sachs, and Merrill Lynch were all on the edge of bankruptcy themselves before the government injected funds into Morgan Stanley and Goldman Sachs, and Merrill Lynch was taken over by Bank of America. These investment banks got into trouble because they relied too heavily on the very short-term overnight repo market to fund their operations. When their asset quality declined, these investment banks did not have sufficient collateral to post to make the short-term overnight repo loans they needed to keep their operations going. The government stepped in and allowed these companies to re-characterize themselves as banks so that they had access to the Federal Reserve's discount window, and our government injected $10 billion of equity into both Goldman Sachs and Morgan Stanley. GMAC received $6 billion worth of investment from the government. GM and Chrysler received some $17 billion just to get them into the first quarter of 2009 and are now seeking tens of billions more.

You will think I'm crazy when I tell you that none of this taxpayer investment had to be made. In every case, the government stepped in and bailed out these companies before the company's creditors and debt investors took a single dollar hit to their investment. The equity investors lost a substantial portion of their investment, but the debt investors were made whole and did not lose a single dime.

It makes no sense for a debt investor who has been enjoying a premium return for decades by investing in these companies and supposedly shouldering the risk of bankruptcy, to get taken out whole and to suffer no loss when the companies do indeed go bankrupt. It makes no sense that the taxpayer who had nothing to do with the operation of these companies and never invested in the debt or equity securities of these companies is asked to come in and make these debt investors whole after they essentially failed. The numbers are quite substantial. If Fannie Mae and Freddie Mac's debt investors had been asked to take just a 15 percent haircut to their investments, no taxpayer monies would have been needed in the initial bailout.

In the case of GMAC, the debt investors were asked to take a 75 percent haircut, but Cerberus, owners of 51 percent of the equity below the debt, were asked only to take a 35 percent haircut. We will look at this transaction in more detail later as this type of structure makes very little sense.

We have said that one of the primary causes of this economic crisis is that all companies, banks included, are too leveraged with debt. The good news, from a workout perspective, is that there are a lot of debt investors that can take a haircut. If a bank is leveraged 20 to 1 with debt and loses 100 percent of its equity it still has 95 percent of its liabilities in the form of depositors and debt investors waiting to take a hit, if needed. Just because a bank loses 5 percent of its assets to bad loans does not mean that they need taxpayer assistance. While no one expects depositors to lose money, it makes no sense to allow creditors and debt investors off the hook.

The other obvious source of funding needed for any substantive restructuring of industry is management compensation. Wall Street, including the investment banks, the commercial banks and the insurance industry, took home executive compensation and bonuses worth more than $500 billion over the last four to five years. Why should they keep these bonuses after they ran their companies into the ground, and expect taxpayers to make up the difference?

It is even worse than that. Many of these companies, even after receiving taxpayer monies in a bailout, continue to pay significant bonuses to their executives. They make a big deal about executives' salaries going to one dollar, but put no limit on stock options and restricted stock grants. Some of these chief executives have said they will not take a bonus for 2009, but they certainly are not returning any of their restricted stock or stock options, and their restriction on cash bonuses only applies to themselves, not to the thousands of management employees in their bank. Chris Dodd added a meaningless addendum to Obama's stimulus bill that restricts bonuses, but not salaries or stock options. Some financial companies that have received bailout monies have announced that their bonus pools are 50 percent lower in 2008 than 2007, but that means that hundreds of billions of dollars of taxpayer money are going to pay bonuses this year to people who made decisions that bankrupted these firms. This makes no sense.

Lie #17 Everything that Hank Paulson ever said about the Troubled Asset Relief Program.

You might be surprised to find comments from Hank Paulson, our country's Treasury secretary, included here in a book about Wall Street lies. But Hank's entire life has been dedicated to Wall Street. And based on his actions as Treasury Secretary, it does not look like he has forgotten his roots.

Hank Paulson told us that the Troubled Asset Relief Program (TARP) would buy underwater mortgage assets so as to free up money for the banks to start lending again. He said he needed $700 billion to accomplish this task. He said he would utilize a reverse auction process in which the government would announce prices at which there were buyers, and then reduce that price until they had people willing to sell them mortgage securities.

It turns out that Hank Paulson and TARP did not buy a single underwater mortgage security. They promptly took the money that was directed to that program and used it in a vast giveaway scheme in which over $300 billion was given to the commercial banks and investment banks, mostly good friends of Hank Paulson.

Paulson had said that these investments would be made on a market-determined basis and they would turn out to be good investments for the taxpayer. Again, far from the truth. While Warren Buffett was able to get a 10 percent preferred on his Goldman Sachs investment, the TARP fund and the US taxpayer only got 5 percent on their preferred investment. And while 100 percent of Warren Buffett's preferred was convertible into the common stock of Goldman Sachs, only 5 percent of the taxpayer's preferred was convertible into common. The GMAC deal was even worse: the preferred was not convertible into common stock, only into more fairly worthless preferred stock.

Even after Paulson admitted that he would never buy underwater securities with the TARP money, he continued to lie about the reason. What he found out too late was that a reverse mortgage auction would never work for mortgage securities. The reason is that mortgage securities are extremely varied in structure and characteristics. Every mortgage deal is different. This means you cannot have a reverse auction for a particular class of mortgage securities because there is no such thing as a class. They are all different. And they are priced accordingly. Paulson has still not admitted that his reverse auction plan was unworkable from the start and that was one of the prime reasons he never pursued buying underwater mortgages with TARP money.

Similarly, what Paulson realized all too late was that buying underwater mortgages from banks would only make the problem worse. Like Bernanke, he thought this was a liquidity problem and he would help the banks by buying their underwater mortgage securities and getting them cash. What he did not realize was that this was a bank solvency crisis and that when the banks sold underwater mortgages, it caused greater losses and a bigger hit to their already weakened equity base. Even if banks decided not to sell into Paulson's hypothetical market for these underwater securities, because Paulson had created a real market price for these bad securities, all the banks would have been forced to mark their securities to that market-determined price, creating greater losses and worsening their solvency crisis.

Paulson also promised that TARP money would only go to troubled institutions, but he ended up giving equity money to J.P. Morgan and other healthy banks, he says, so as not to taint companies that received TARP money. While he promised that only federally regulated banks would receive money, he quickly allowed Goldman Sachs and Morgan Stanley to re-characterize themselves as banks and eventually even ended up calling GMAC a regulated bank. It is inexplicable how he justifies giving car companies such as GM and Chrysler TARP money when the whole idea of TARP was to help financial institutions.

Finally, Paulson lied when he said that these investments of taxpayer money would be closely monitored. Harvard Law School's Elizabeth Warren heads a commission that is supervising the TARP funding and that has come out with a number of very critical reports stating that the government has done a very poor job of monitoring any of these investments with little to no reporting to the taxpayers of what has happened to their money. Paulson used TARP like his own private piggy bank and has doled out more than $350 billion to companies of his choosing. There is no rhyme or reason to who receives funds and who does not. We have wasted $350 billion plus of our hard-earned taxpayer money and we have nothing to show for it. The mortgage crisis is not abating, housing prices continue to decline, foreclosures continue to increase, the credit markets are still frozen, the interbank lending rate is still high and more and more companies face bankruptcy. Paulson has wasted more than a third of a trillion dollars of taxpayer money.

Lie #18 There are a few select large financial institutions that are the foundation of our banking system and, as such, are too big and important to fail.

Another lie that Paulson has promulgated is that there are a few very large financial institutions that are the foundation of our banking system, and that by definition are too big to fail. This is how he justified giving hundreds of billions of dollars to the commercial banking and investment banking industry.

It is true that there are institutions in America that are so big and so interconnected in our financial markets that their failure would trigger a collapse of the entire financial system. But the number of such institutions is not limited to just a half dozen. There are hundreds if not thousands of such firms.

For decades, financial institutions in this country were allowed to grow to such sizes that they measured their assets and liabilities in the trillions of dollars. These institutions by themselves were so large and so interconnected with the global economy that if they failed, the global economy would fail. Why didn't someone think of this sooner? Why didn't we do something about restricting the size of our largest financial institutions?

We would not have to pass an anti-growth legislation. Rather, we could insist that every time a financial institution got to $200 billion in shareholder equity or $500 billion in assets, it would be split into two new companies and shareholders would get shares in each of the new companies in exchange for the old. There would be no diminution of value. No one would be worse off. But the system would be protected from having some institutions grow to such a size that we could not allow them to fail.

Once companies get to a size where they cannot fail, capitalism breaks down. Capitalism is all about giving entrepreneurs the opportunity to build businesses and increase profits and grow on the small end. But it is also, especially amongst big companies, all about allowing poorly-run companies to fail. There has to be creative destruction in capitalism. Poorly-run companies making bad management decisions are getting out scot-free. Instead they have to be allowed to fail in order for well-run companies to increase their market share and profitability.

But it was not just the very large financial institutions that were too big to fail. Because of the credit default swap market, almost every financial institution in the world was actually too big, or at least too important a node in the CDS market, to fail. The credit default swap market is a $65 trillion derivatives market in which companies insure each other against default. In essence, in the credit default swap market, I can guarantee you that IBM will not fail, and if it does I will make you whole on your IBM debt investments.

The credit default swap market was allowed to grow, over the last ten years, completely unregulated and completely without transparency from a $140 billion market to a $65 trillion market today. It is a vast interconnected spider web of two counterparty transactions in which one party guarantees defaults and the other receives payment in case of a company's collapse.

None of the big financial players in the credit default swap market, and here I mean almost every single big financial player in the world, can be allowed to fail under such an interconnected spider web of guarantees regarding bankruptcy. The reason is that the company's bankruptcy will trigger payments under the credit default swap market. Secondly, the financial institution that fails is a counterparty in the credit default swap market to lots of other guarantees, so a great deal of contracts will collapse. The entire spider web of interconnected guarantees and insurance products implicit in the credit default swap market collapses if any of the major nodes fail.

A beautiful analogy to see the importance of nodes in an interconnected system is to imagine what would happen if the Chicago airport closed for a couple of hours due to snowfall. Not only would flights be delayed in cities that service Chicago, but flights across the whole country would immediately be delayed and many canceled. You cannot project the severe consequences of losing a major node in an interconnected network, such as an airport or the credit default swap market; the system is so complex as to become completely unpredictable during failures and outages.

Lie #19 We can save the auto industry with a $17 billion bailout by government.

The auto industry approached our government with the request to be bailed out. Weekly the amount of money they were requesting changed. The figure initially agreed on of $17 billion was far from adequate.

This was an industry that was losing close to $25 billion every quarter. It is always bad business to fund a company's continuing operating losses as an investment strategy. By giving the auto industry $17 billion, all we were doing was delaying making a decision about whether to allow it to go bankrupt and restructure or to go out of business. That decision would be no easier two months later. Sure enough, in February 2009 GM and Chrysler came back to request another $20-plus billion in aid.

The American auto industry is fundamentally broken in almost every way companies can be. It takes six to seven years to introduce a new model and their new car designs are often rejected by the market. It has never offered innovation in increasing miles per gallon standards or in introducing electric vehicles or hybrids. It has probably three times as many dealerships as it needs, and Americans find approaching a car dealership to buy a car to be one of the most unpleasant experiences in their lives.

Workers' pay structure is too high as they earn approximately 20 to 30 percent more than American workers employed at Japanese car companies in the States. Almost all of the cash flow generated by the business goes to paying retiree pension and health care benefits. It is the nature of this problem that regardless of how much you shrink these companies, funding the retiree costs only gets worse. It is why these businesses so desperately need to be restructured.

Barack Obama very much wants to have a vibrant American auto industry and avoid the spike in unemployment that would result if these American car companies went out of business. But it makes no sense to invest additional taxpayer money until these companies are completely restructured. Their creditors need to take a substantial hit to their investment, their equity investors need to be wiped out, their management teams need replacing, their factory workers' pay has to be adjusted downward, their retirees' pension and health care plans must be reduced in cost, dealerships have to be closed, and the number of car models must be significantly reduced.

By the time the American taxpayer is done trying to save these three companies they will have invested over $100 billion. Such a substantial sum is enough to start an entire new auto industry under better management with the incentive to produce higher mileage cars and electric vehicles. For $100 billion we can turn the entire country on to electric vehicles with an added new emphasis on mass transit and electric buses.

This is a classic example of throwing good money after bad. It will not work. It is a complete waste of taxpayer money.

Lie #20 Banks are more stable than investment banks because of their stable deposit base; therefore, it makes sense to turn investment banks, CIT, and GMAC into bank holding companies.

Investment banks like Bear Stearns and Lehman Brothers and eventually Merrill Lynch, Goldman Sachs, and Morgan Stanley were all threatened with bankruptcy even quicker than the commercial banks. The reason given was that commercial banks face less risk because they have a more stable depositor base, while the investment banks must depend on the markets each night for their financing.

As we have seen, it is true the investment banks depend far too much on very short-term overnight financing to run their businesses. Each of them borrows hundreds of billions of dollars on an overnight basis in the repurchase or repo markets. If anything should go wrong with the investment bank, or rumors should swell about potential problems, or if they should fail to find sufficient collateral to post in the repo market, or if the repo market itself should face a temporary crisis, any of these investment banks could disappear in a flash.

In contrast, banks typically have customer deposits that make up as much as 60 to 90 percent of the liabilities side of the balance sheet. Some of these deposits are demand deposits in that they reflect checking accounts in which the funds can be withdrawn at any time. Much of these deposits are of slightly longer-term certificates of deposit or CDs that mature in anywhere from three months to five years.

But the real reason why commercial bank deposits are a more stable source of funding is because commercial bank deposits are guaranteed by the United States government. Before this crisis, up to $100,000 was guaranteed. Now $250,000 in bank deposits per account is guaranteed by the US government.

This is not necessarily a good thing. If one seeks a big picture perspective on the current crisis, one could argue that the banks themselves are faced with a moral hazard question; regardless of how risky the assets they position or businesses they enter, they know their deposit base would never flee because of its government guarantee. This is the same kind of thinking that got Fannie Mae and Freddie Mac in trouble. They had an implied guarantee from the government on all their borrowing. It led them to increase leverage on their companies in excess of 100 to 1 and eventually buy subprime mortgages in the secondary market.

So it is a mistake to say that commercial banks are better financed than the investment banks because of their stable depositor base. If you take away the government guarantees, the banks would be subject to bank runs if they did stupid things in the future. Northern Rock, the eighth largest bank in England, found that out when depositors lined up around the block and removed $2 billion in a single day, effectively bankrupting the company, which forced its takeover by the government.

So we have a rush of investment banks, auto finance companies and consumer finance companies like Goldman Sachs, GMAC, and CIT reorganizing and claiming to be commercial banks so that their deposits can be guaranteed by the government. I do not see how this can be good for the financial system or the economy. Once again, we have taken one of the primary reasons for the crisis, in this case the moral hazard that banks face due to the government guarantee of their deposits, and have expanded it to non-bank institutions as a partial solution to the crisis.

We shall see in later chapters that the problems that got us into this mess are being magnified in the suggested solutions to the crisis. For example, much of this crisis was a result of too much borrowing and consuming by individuals, businesses, and the government, in a low interest rate environment. So today, what is the attempted solution to this problem? A near zero percent interest rate set by the Fed, dramatic increases in government borrowing and government spending, tax cuts, and fiscal stimuli funded by more government debt to encourage ever greater consumer spending.

Investment Strategy Lies

Lie #21 Diversification is the key. If everyone held a broadly diversified portfolio, the markets and society would be much more stable, efficient, and productive.

If you learn but one thing at business school it is that investors should always diversify. Investors can minimize their risk exposure and maximize their portfolio returns through diversification.

A presumed corollary suggests that if everybody diversified, total returns for the entire world would be maximized at a minimum of risk and the world would be better off. But is this true?

Greater diversification is recommended for investors because the volatility of the entire portfolio is reduced. But problems do result if everyone follows this advice.

To be well diversified, an investor must hold not only almost every stock in the United States, he must hold stocks in every country of the world. In addition, he should hold all asset classes in addition to stocks. He should hold commodities, bonds, real estate, and so on in the proportion that these assets make up the total wealth of the world.

This creates quite a conundrum for a typical institutional investor. Imagine a German bank that wants to fully diversify its portfolio. First of all, they have to buy thousands of stocks around the world, hundreds of different commodities and real assets, and hold thousands of real estate positions. The transaction costs alone would overwhelm the company.

Besides the transaction costs, the first question that is raised in trying to implement such a diversification strategy is how can a single investment manager at a German bank be expected to be knowledgeable about all the assets in the world and their pricing. He can't be. He knows that in order to properly diversify he should invest a portion of his portfolio in US mortgage securities, but he knows nothing about US mortgages and their risk of default.

This does not stop him from buying US mortgage securities. He takes great comfort in the efficient markets theory, which says that all assets and securities in a market are properly priced by the market itself to account for the risk attached to them. In other words, when you go to buy IBM's stock in the market you do not need to do any fundamental analysis or research on IBM, because the market price incorporates all the best information and the best research work on IBM.

You can see the problem that develops. If everyone in the world develops this approach they end up investing in assets they know nothing about with the assumption that someone else is doing the fundamental research necessary to make sure that it is a good investment. Even if they wanted to, the sheer number of assets and securities that they have to hold in order to be properly diversified prevents them from doing a detailed securities analysis on each of their investments.

As a natural outgrowth of this diversification phenomenon, you would expect an entire industry of middlemen to be created to assist these investors with their investment decisions on assets they know little about. And this is just what we have seen. There are research companies that provide information on pretty much any asset or security in the world, investment banks that give their opinion as to value, rating agencies that provide ratings under the assumption you don't need to do much critical analysis if the security is rated AAA, financial advisers, and so on.

In addition, funds are created that invest in entire broad classes of securities. For example, the German bank investment manager may decide to invest in a fund that holds a broad array of commercial real estate properties in the United States rather than trying to own these properties directly. But the introduction of these funds and funds of funds adds additional transaction costs and makes investing more costly. One and 2 percent annual fees do not sound that big until you realize that the real return on risk-free securities over time has only been 2 to 3 percent per year.

The major problem with introducing so many middlemen to the investment decision is that you end up not knowing whom to trust. These middlemen do not necessarily lose money when your portfolio goes down in value. As a matter of fact, most of these fund managers care more about performance relative to their peers in the industry than they do about the absolute performance of your fund investments. For example, if the stock market goes down 20 percent and I am an investment manager running a pool of money that only goes down 15 percent, I am applauded and rewarded with additional monies to invest in the coming year. But if you had invested your assets with me, you would still have an absolute loss of 15 percent. This emphasis on relative rather than absolute returns can encourage managers to just follow the market and invest in momentum plays on the upside, and to ride downturns with a buy-and-hold strategy as long as everyone else is doing the same thing.

But again, the real problem with middlemen, as evidenced in the current financial crisis, is the question of whether they can be trusted. As the manager of my own assets, I know that my objective is to maximize the value of those assets with the minimum of risk. It is not clear that the middlemen created through a broad diversification strategy share the same objective. Fund managers may be trying to attract capital to their funds by achieving good relative performance, with little concern for real losses I am suffering. Investment banks may be trying to please their corporate issuing clients by getting them a good price for their new securities. Or investment banks may be selling assets that are overvalued because their principal investing arm is dumping them. Another group of infamous middlemen, the rating agencies, are paid by the issuer, and the sheer volume of new issues, and in recent years the exorbitant fees paid to the rating agencies, clearly caused them to lose their perspective on what really warrants a AAA rating. You may turn to a commercial bank for investment advice, especially about derivatives, but will be disappointed to learn that their advice is tainted by their trying to hedge their own derivatives exposure.

Possibly the most damaging side effect of diversification, if you can call something which destroys the entire global financial system a side effect, is that investors end up holding so many company assets and securities that they cannot police the individual companies and managements. If I hold 1,000 stocks in an attempt to be properly diversified, where would I find the time to police the managements of each to be sure they are working in the shareholders' best interest?

The most obvious example of this has occurred with regard to executive pay. People are shocked to learn that the Fortune 500 companies on average pay their CEOs tens of millions of dollars a year, or approximately 350 times what the average worker earns. Free-market advocates said that this needed no policing because executive pay was subject to approval by the company's board of directors. Even if the board of directors were totally independent and representative of shareholders' interests, because every investor is well diversified each company ends up having hundreds of thousands of investors. Because each investor has thousands of different investments under their diversification strategy, none of them have the time to police the executive pay at each of their portfolio companies.

And this is really just the tip of the iceberg. Companies end up unsupervised and poorly managed because shareholders do not have the time to actively police their investments. Big publicly traded companies are notoriously poorly-run. You need only look at the American auto companies who have been mismanaged for forty years with no effort on behalf of their shareholders to straighten out their managements.

There is additional proof in the marketplace that this problem is very severe. The proof is that private equity firms can take publicly traded companies private and create greater value than that of the publicly traded company. This should violate what we know of finance because we know that publicly traded stocks have greater liquidity and require lower returns for holding them. All things being equal, if you take a publicly traded stock private, your private investors should demand a higher return due to their lesser liquidity, which means that if the cash flow from the companies does not change, the value of the company has to go down. In other words, all other things being equal, a company should be worth less, not more, when you take it private. But we are seeing just the opposite in the marketplace. Private equity firms pay premiums to the publicly traded stock price to buy companies, then make very good returns for their investors, even though they bought the companies at inflated prices.

You'll notice that in the preceding paragraph I was careful to qualify my argument with "all other things being equal." Of course, all other things are not kept equal. What happens when a company goes private is that you remove the hundreds of thousands of shareholders and reduce ownership to a single owner: the sponsoring private equity firm. Now the owner has the time that is required to successfully police the management of the company and assure that the company is run to maximize return to shareholders, not enrich managements. These big, sloppily run, publicly traded companies become lean, mean, fighting machines as private companies, and they create enormous profits for their private equity fund sponsors.

This is a wonderful example in the real world of how the theory of diversification has led to greater inefficiencies, not greater efficiencies, in the market. No one is watching the collective shops of our largest companies. We have introduced so many middlemen—including the executive managements of the companies themselves, who each have their own personal objectives that do not necessarily involve maximizing value to shareholders—that we find that cash flows and profits are not maximized, and values and investments are harmed.

The entire theory of diversification should not be thrown out. But it should be greatly modified. A good investor should hold a portfolio of twenty or thirty stocks and assets that she or he can keep a very close eye on and thoroughly understand, and then supervise managements to ensure that shareholder interests are honored. The use of middlemen should be greatly reduced.

The world's belief that greater diversification leads to greater investment returns with lower risk may have significantly contributed to the current financial crisis. When you cut through it, the investment manager at the German commercial bank had no valid reason to be investing in extremely complex US mortgage securities like CDOs. He knew nothing about them and he brought no value added by investing. And he ended up getting punished.

There is one final point I should make about diversification. As investors around the world insist on greater diversification, their fortunes become more interconnected and intertwined. You see this most dramatically in the credit default swap market. Investors tried to diversify and share the risk of bankruptcy, or default across a number of institutions. What they ended up doing was creating a world in which any single large company's default would trigger losses of such magnitude through the system that it would trigger an entire string of defaults and cause a financial catastrophe.

Globalization has clearly added to this interconnectedness. Remember when Thailand got the Asian flu, Russia came down with it, and Long-Term Capital Management (LTCM) went bankrupt? I titled my previous book on the financial crisis *Contagion*, and when you see how infectious global financial problems are and how quickly they spread between countries and various asset markets, you begin to understand how diversification can create the very problem it was meant to solve, namely controlling risk.

Lie #22 Buy low–sell high is a tried and true, guaranteed investment strategy.

At first blush, it's hard to argue with such a blatantly obvious statement of how to achieve superior returns as an investor. This is a classic example of Monday morning quarterbacking. As we look back at the historical record of an individual stock, we wish we had bought the stock at its all-time low and sold at its all-time high. This strategy would have made a great deal of money for us.

The problem, of course, is identifying the highs and lows in real time as they are occurring, not after the fact. This is nearly impossible. To prove this, pick five stocks you think are currently at their all-time high or all-time low currently. I would guess that over six months you will have been proved wrong in every case.

The problem in identifying highs and lows is that you are picking inflection points; you are identifying the precise time when a general trend downward reverses or when a general trend upward turns north. A stock may trade up twenty days in a row. Imagine how difficult it is to predict that on the twenty-first day, it will turn down.

Many times stocks that have been trading up each day take a pause and then trade level or slightly down. It would be very easy to make the mistake and assume that this is the top. Often, after a brief pause, or slight decline, the stock continues its upward climb, and if you sold you would have missed this extra appreciation.

We shall see in the discussion below on technical research and investing that there is little new information in the historical price trend of the stock that is not already incorporated in its price. If stock investing were as easy as buying those stocks that had trended upward historically in the expectation they would continue to increase, we would all be billionaires.

The fact of the matter is that there is very little real trending in stocks. Again, looking at the historical record or chart for individual stocks, it appears that there are lots of smooth curves and trends upward and downward in the stock. But a completely randomly generated pattern would have the same sorts of smooth ups and downs that appear to be trends. Remember, randomness does not occur like one heads, one tails, one heads, one tails, one heads. Rather, randomness looks like three heads followed by two tails followed by four heads followed by one tail followed by one head followed by six tails. After the fact, you can find highs and lows in the randomly generated string of data, but by definition, there is no such actual high and low that would have been predictable in the random sequence.

My personal belief is that for many reasons the stock market is not perfect, and is subject to bubbles and busts. For this reason, as an investment philosophy, I would more heavily weight my purchases toward those periods in which the stock market appears to be dramatically undervalued relative to a major yardstick like revenues. Over time, the stock market seems to fluctuate between approximately 0.6 times revenues and 2.0 times revenues. I would be a general buyer below 1.0 times revenues and a general seller above 1.5 times revenues. I utilize revenues rather than earnings because earnings themselves are much too volatile given business cycles and bubbles.

workforce. Not only will we lose their productive efforts, but they will continue to age, requiring much greater state assistance with their retirement and health care. This cannot be good for the economy.

Lie #24 A buy-and-hold long-term investing strategy yields superior returns over trying to sell in down markets.

In November of 2007, with the stock market near its all-time high and trading just shy of 14,000, I gave a talk to approximately 200 investors in my parents' hometown in Kentucky. I told those investors that the stock market typically moves first and trades off before difficult economic climates develop. In this case, for whatever reason, bad economic times were already being exposed in the housing, mortgage, home building and banking sectors, and yet the stock market had not begun to trade down.

I told these investors that this was the stock market's Christmas present to them. The stock market, in effect, was giving these investors the opportunity to get out before company earnings and company stock prices declined. I then gave them an hour presentation on how bad the coming recession might be. I concluded by saying that even if they did not believe my forecast, it made no sense for them to hold common stocks given the substantial risk of a very severe recession and very little upside in the economy or in the stock market.

Just being risk averse, they should have taken money out of the stock market; they clearly did not know the direction of the future economy, and they only needed to read the newspapers at the time to realize there was a very real threat of a significant downturn.

Imagine my surprise when my two cousins, who are both lawyers in Louisville, came up to me after the presentation and, after congratulating me on making my case that the economy was weakening, told me that they did not intend to sell any of their stocks. Their reasoning? They said they were buy-and-hold investors who believed that selling into every piece of bad news ended up not only achieving low prices on the sale, but typically caused them to miss any future rebounds in the stock market.

If you look at a historic record of the United States stock market, this again appears to be a successful strategy. The reason, quite simply, is that the United States has been the big winner in the world economy. When you look at the historical record, every time the US stock market has declined, it has bounced back. But just because this has occurred historically does not mean it's always going to be true. If you grew up in a country other than the United States you would see that this is not necessarily the case. There are many examples of countries' stock markets declining and their currencies weakening, and rather than bouncing back they continue to decline until the countries bankrupt themselves and default on their debts.

So, while I could not fault the logic of my cousins' buy-and-hold investment strategy, one should realize that it is not infallible. Certainly we hope the United States is not going to go bankrupt because of the current crisis, but this does not mean that the stock market might not trade down and stay there for a long period of time. If the stock market trades in the 5,000 to 9,000 range for ten years, you will wish that you had not bought and held, but rather sold and invested in assets that had a greater upside and a greater return potential in the future.

I believe, even at the currently depressed levels for the Dow Jones industrial, there is still too much downside risk to be fully invested in US stocks. I cannot think of another country that I would want to be invested in, with the possible exception of China if one took a very long-term view. This means that for the next eighteen months to two years it might be best to hold your investment monies in cash, very short-term Treasury securities, Treasury Inflation-Protected Securities (TIPS), and gold. The key during a downturn is not to earn an unusually high return on your money, it is to get your money back. Ideally, you would like to get your principal back and have its purchasing power protected from inflation. Given that inflation may reignite as the countries of the world print money to stimulate their economies, short Treasuries, TIPS and gold seem like logical places to invest.

Lie #25 Dollar cost averaging, or buying in over time in small purchases, is a great way to achieve good returns without subjecting yourself to the risk of large losses.

You hear this investment strategy often from stockbrokers, investment advisors, and even television personalities like Jim Cramer. This strategy can be summarized thus: if you are not certain about a particular investment, then rather than allotting the full amount that you want to invest, say $10,000, you invest only a quarter, say $2,500. Then if you are wrong, and the stock trades further down, you can invest another $2,500 at what is supposedly a better price. As the stock continues to trade down you can continue to invest $2,500 over time until your full $10,000 is invested.

By doing the investment in increments, you have successfully limited the very large loss that would have occurred if you had invested $10,000 initially. You also have a lower basis in your investment, which is the average price of all of your $2,500 investments, than if you had invested $10,000 initially.

Of course, there is no such thing as a free lunch in economics. By not investing the full $10,000, you miss the opportunity to earn a large return if the stock immediately goes up. By only investing $2,500 initially, you only have $2,500 at work of your $10,000 stake.

If $10,000 was your total investment pool under this strategy you will have only invested 25 percent of your investment monies initially. The presumption is that the other 75 percent will have to be held in cash and earn cash-like returns. The blended return—25 percent in stock and 75 percent cash—would be a poor return if the stock market increased.

The other way to see the fallacy in this investment strategy is to look at each of the $2,500 investments you make. If this strategy made sense, then why wouldn't it make sense to break each of these $2,500 investments into four $625 investments, and postpone making the full $2,500 investment just like you postponed the $10,000 investment? You can see where this leads. If the strategy made sense, rather than making an investment in a stock you like, you would end up spreading the investment over a long period of time into infinitesimally small investments. What would be the advantage of that?

You should never invest more in a particular stock than you can afford to lose. But, if you like the stock, and you have done good analytical research, then when it is time to buy, it is time to buy. If you think it might be better to wait, that is fine, just don't make the investment until you are comfortable with the timing. Wait for the price to come down further and then invest the full amount. But this idea that you can save money by layering your investment out over time is not true. The foregone profit opportunity if the market improves exactly equals your cost savings if the situation deteriorates.

Lie #26 Life-cycle investing means that people save during their productive years and then consume during their retirement years.

This is a very famous tenet of investing theory. It was made famous by Milton Friedman who wrote a number of famous papers on the life-cycle theory of investing. But is it true?

Certainly looking at America over the last ten years, the theory does not seem to hold. Americans have saved less each year, and now the savings rate in the United States is negative. In the country as a whole, until very recently, there have been no savings occurring and people have been consuming more than they make, so they are going into increasing debt through negative savings.

For a time, this might have been explained by the rapid rise in home prices. People began to feel that they didn't have to save because their homes were increasing so rapidly in price. Their homes became not only their ATM machines, where they could withdraw cash for other purchases, they became their retirement plans.

It is doubly surprising that this lack of savings occurred in America during a period when most Americans lost their defined benefit pension plans. Only 10 percent of working Americans now have a defined benefit pension plan, down from 60 percent at its peak. This means that many are relying on defined contribution plans like 401(k)s and Social Security to pay for their retirement.

But many Americans are putting little money into their 401(k)s. And as we all know, Social Security is going bankrupt and will not be able to fund substantial retirement costs in the future. Health care costs are exploding, and yet Americans are not making any provision for payment of their health care needs as they age.

Not only is there little to no savings going on in America, but it is a fallacy that the elderly are consuming their savings. As a matter of fact, the elderly's assets continue to grow. Households headed by people over sixty-five years in age have approximately $270,000 in assets, and this number has grown over time. Rather than saving during their lifetime and consuming that savings in retirement, in America the elderly's savings have continued to grow.

This should set off a warning bell that all is not right with the economic foundations of America. Just as it makes no sense for a poor country like China to be saving 40 percent of its income and lending it out for a rich country like the United States to consume, it makes little sense for younger workers to be saving nothing for their own retirement and yet paying 13 percent of their wages to the elderly, whose savings are growing. The average working American aged twenty to forty years old has less than $30,000 in savings, and yet he is spending 13 percent of his income in the form of Social Security payments to the elderly, who have $275,000 in savings, on average.

You cannot have a healthy economy if your young productive workers are being so penalized that they cannot afford to save and invest. Much of the productive capacity of the country is owned by the elderly. It cannot be good for our country to have such a dramatic difference in generational wealth. As a matter of fact, people over fifty-five years old in America control nearly 85 percent of the wealth of America.

The Social Security system and the entire economy must be transformed so that younger workers have the motivation to work hard, save for their retirement, and invest in their country's future. Simply transferring their wealth to elders without saving for their own retirement does nothing to encourage a healthy and vibrant, growing economy.

Lie #27 Technical analysis involving the charting of the historical prices of stocks can be very helpful in identifying buying opportunities or recognizing critical selling signals.

Technical analysis is nothing more than examining a graph of a particular stock's historical price movements to see if you can uncover patterns in the movement of the stock that will help you predict its direction in the future.

While the language of technical analysis is very sophisticated, it is the lowest form of fundamental research one can do. If the stock appears to be trending upward each day, a technical analyst might suggest buying the stock and riding the stock's momentum. But that can't be all there is to successful stock investing. Any third grader can draw a trendline by connecting dots. If the fortunes of a company were expected to improve every day or every week or every year, you would not expect the stock to gradually increase in a general trendline upward over time, you would expect the stock price to jump reflecting the net present value of that future prosperity. And once the stock jumps and reflects people's expectations that the earning prospects will be good, there will be no reason for the stock to trend upward further. Therefore, if you see a stock trending upwards, it is most likely an illusion. It is probably caused by randomness, as even random numbers appear to trend up and down over time.

Of course, with perfect hindsight, we can identify winning stocks that actually have trended upward over a long period of time. But we can also identify, after the fact, those stocks that have trended downward over time. The trick is separating them, not after the fact, but in advance. Google may be a very good company with a very good business plan and a very good outlook for its earnings, but this does not mean that the stock price has to go up in the future. Its stock price already reflects all that good information, and when you purchase Google at its trading price today there should be an equal probability of Google stock price in the future going up or going down.

Similarly, when a technical analyst suggests that he has looked at the stock price history of a particular company and determined that there is buying support at a particular lower price and suggests that it is unlikely the stock will go through that level, he is doing nothing more than reading tea leaves. What he is suggesting is that at the lower stock price there is a group of investors who are open to buy the stock at that price and will support it. But he knows no such thing. Rather he is just constructing an attractive story based on a historical price graph.

You need only read a single book on charting or technical analysis or listen to a technical analyst speak about the markets to understand how worthless all of their advice is. The ultimate test I would love to give a technical chartist is to show him a historical price graph of actual stocks and ask him to predict what will happen in the future. We can then track his predictions to see if they have any real value.

Another fun exercise would be to show a technical analyst a randomly generated stream of data over time, tell him it was the stock price for a particular company, and see what he predicts the future will hold. I guarantee you that even in randomness, he will begin to see heads, shoulders, patterns and trends that are not really there.

There is a more modern reason why some finance professionals believe that stocks can trend over time. They believe that very large investing institutions are so big that when they decide to unload a position in a particular stock, they must do it over a period of time so as not to impact the stock price dramatically. I can tell you from experience that there are very sophisticated filtering programs on Wall Street that use cutting-edge technology to try to uncover any weekly trend patterns, and when they find them, they arbitrage the results and eliminate them. It is very doubtful that an individual investor would be able to uncover such hidden trends in the data without very sophisticated computer analysis. Certainly technical chartists can't see these hidden trends armed only with a chart and a laser pointer.

Lie #28 Before investing, you should talk with a financial advisor whose professionalism and long-term investing perspective will end up saving you a great deal of money over time.

There are many examples of professionals, such as doctors, dentists, and lawyers, who work hard their entire life and then turn over their life savings to a stockbroker to invest. The world has gotten more specialized, so it is not unusual to find very smart doctors and lawyers who know next to nothing about finance and the stock market.

They assume that getting professional advice will ensure success in their investing portfolio. But the first rule of efficient markets says that no one can beat the market. It's difficult to track all the investment advice given by stockbrokers, but academic studies have been done as to the quality of their research departments' advice and it has been found to offer next to nothing in value. Over time, buying the stocks that banks' research departments recommend does not yield any abnormal or superior performance in a portfolio.

Similarly, a study was done in which all of Jim Cramer's investment advice was followed, and it was determined that he did not outperform the market either.

Finally, a study of all mutual funds shows that in aggregate they also underperform the market by exactly the amount of their fees. Similarly, it appears that more than half the hedge funds in the world will close or go bankrupt in this current financial crisis and that after adjusting for risk across all hedge funds, there is no abnormal return. Private equity firms such as Blackstone and Fortress have seen their common stock prices drop by 70 to 80 percent.

If no one can beat the market, then it makes no sense to pay 1, 2, or 3 percent fees per year to get worthless advice. Rather, most people should just invest their money in a general index fund like Vanguard that has very low fees and just replicates the overall stock market return.

If you are not going to put your money in a general index fund, than I would recommend picking twenty stocks that you have reason to believe are good investments and holding them. But you should have a very good reason for investing in each stock or you should not be in the stock market. If you don't have a view on a particular stock and you don't have any special information that the stock is undervalued, then you are wasting your time investing in the stock market. Just because the stock market has increased in the past does not mean it will increase in the future. Maybe your educated view is that America will do well in the future relative to other countries, and if this is your belief then maybe holding a broad index of American stocks makes sense even if you have little knowledge of individual company stock valuations.

Of course, even in a world where all hedge funds and all mutual funds on average underperform the market, each year there will be stellar performers that outperform their peers. And it is the nature of investing that these stellar investors will attract greater monies to invest in the future. But it is not true that historical investment performance is a good predictor of future performance. This latest market crash exposed a number of supposed great investment gurus who had done very well for twenty- and twenty-five-year periods only to find their entire funds bankrupted by the current financial crisis. It's very easy to generate excess returns if you're willing to bet against a very severe crisis occurring in the financial markets. People will pay you to insure against such a crisis. You will make money every year—like AIG—but if a crisis occurs you will go bankrupt—like AIG.

When inflation was running at 10 to 15 percent per year, portfolios had to grow at 15 to 20 percent just to stay even after taxes. People got used to charging 2 and 3 percent fees to manage your money. But in a world of zero inflation, a 3 percent return per year would be a very good real return, and to give 1 or 2 percent of that to your financial advisor seems like awfully expensive advice, advice that most likely has very little real value associated with it.

Stock Investing Lies

Lie #29 In the long run, stocks outperform bonds if you do not object to slightly higher volatility along the way.

I cannot tell you how many times over the years I have heard this old adage, that in the long run stocks outperform bonds if you do not mind slightly more volatility in your returns.

It is a complete misstatement of the difference between stocks and bonds. Yes, stocks are more volatile than bonds, but there is nothing in finance that suggests that just because they're more volatile they are certain to return a greater profit in the long term.

What finance theory says is that because stocks are more volatile, people will require a higher expected rate of return from them—the key word in the sentence being "expected." Because stocks have high volatility, there is a wide variance of actual outcomes possible around this expected performance.

Many cite this adage in trying to convince younger Americans to invest in the stock market today. The argument goes something like this: Well, I'm fifty-eight years old and I plan on retiring in seven years, and so as the market trades down in the short term it may have an impact on the life savings I need to live on in retirement. But you, a young person in your twenties or thirties, have no immediate need for your savings. You could withstand a temporary downturn in the stock market and when it recovers you will do fine in retirement. And then comes the nail in the coffin. You see, in the long term, stocks always outperform bonds.

Betting on the stock market rather than holding bonds is a bit like taking on the risk of flipping a coin to see what your future wealth will be. Assume a heads flip of the coin means that the stock market goes up and a tails means the stock market goes down. Certainly if you were five or ten years away from retirement, you would not want to risk a significant amount of your assets in the stock market because there is some probability that three tails may come up in a row and you will watch as your life savings are wiped out. For a younger person, three tails could come up initially, followed by two heads, followed by one tail, followed by two heads, and in the long run you would hope that the stock market would achieve its higher expected return rather than bonds.

But there is no guarantee of this. That is why it's called an expected return. There are lots of states of the world, lots of coin flips, in which stocks end up underperforming bonds. Of course, this is not the glamorous story of a high-growth, stable country; rather it is the story of a country in decline in which other countries of the world take over the mantle of being the world leader. But if this is the fate that the United States faces, I don't think that it will come slowly. I think it will come, like all other news, rather suddenly. Today, the United States supposedly has $11 trillion of debt, up from $5 trillion of debt just eight years ago. But the real number might be closer to $18 trillion when all of the guarantees that Paulson and Bernanke put out into the marketplace to try to cure this crisis are recognized. In addition, there is another $30 trillion of unfunded liabilities for Social Security and Medicare. So what was a stated $5 trillion debt eight years ago may be close to a $50 trillion liability exposure today. For a $14 trillion GDP country, with its GDP shrinking quite possibly 10 to 20 percent in the near future, and an annual operating deficit of $2 trillion, you can paint a scenario where foreign lenders like China might just stop lending to the United States. If this happens, either Americans have to very quickly start saving in the middle of a recession, or the Federal Reserve has to start printing money to pay its bills, causing inflation that will severely damage the economy and cause further stock market declines.

So, there is no guarantee that in the long run stocks will outperform bonds. And if you believe that the current financial difficulties of the United States and its economy will continue for eight to ten years, even young people should not be investing in this market. Even though they are making a forty- to fifty-year investment, why would they accept negative returns for the first ten years of that investment horizon? As a matter of fact, if they do, it is very difficult to get the math to work where they would have an adequate amount of money to retire in the future.

Lie #30 Stock market crashes are impossible today because markets are efficient; they properly and rationally price securities with all relevant information, making large one-day movements nearly impossible.

I went to business school at UCLA's Anderson School of Management, which is very much in the University of Chicago tradition that teaches that markets are efficient—that is, that stocks are properly valued in the marketplace. And, mostly, I believe this to be true.

Every week some academic in the world writes a research paper trying to claim that the markets are inefficient, that human behavior is more important than logic in determining stock prices, that people's foibles can be reflected in stock prices, or that the market is too subject to the very real human emotions of panic and fear.

Mostly I discount these findings because I see a stock market that almost always properly reflects the true values and earning potentials of the underlying companies. There has also been an enormous amount of academic literature debunking these attacks on the market's efficiency.

There are times when the stock market does do crazy things. Of course, the two most recent examples are the high-tech boom and the housing boom. In some ways, the high-tech boom was more threatening to efficient market theory because it affected publicly traded stocks on major stock exchanges, which are very liquid and very sophisticated. This is a much more damning indictment of efficient markets than to say that homes in Phoenix were over-priced for some period of time. While the home market in Phoenix is a fairly liquid market, it is nowhere near as sophisticated as the stock exchanges around the world.

Of course, after the fact, everybody understands that not all high-tech companies could be worth as much as Microsoft or Cisco. But even during the high-tech boom, it seemed crazy to assign such large values to high-tech companies given that by the very nature of their business they face great obsolescence risk in their products. The fact that technology is innovating so quickly means that even market leaders, such as Yahoo, can quickly be threatened by new technology and new companies, such as Google. As a matter of fact, that is why I think Google is overvalued today. They hold a very dominant position, not only in search, but in online advertising, which is bankrupting traditional advertising venues in newspapers and media, and yet their valuation seems to presuppose that they will be the technological and market leader for a very long time.

Remember, the value of a common stock is the net present value of all of its future dividends to its shareholders. There is no question that Google will earn a substantial amount of money in the short-term and make generous dividend payments to shareholders. The question for Google is whether they will be in business long enough to continue to make dividend payments to justify their current stock price. Won't another Google come along with a better search engine and bankrupt the original?

What I noticed in 1999 was that many high-tech companies were depending on banner ads on their websites to generate cash flow for their companies. But banner ads cost a nickel at that time for 1,000 banner ads. This means that a $1 million advertising budget would purchase 20 billion banner ads. There is no way that a technology company dependent on banner ads for its revenue source could ever justify being worth hundreds of billions of dollars.

The inefficiency I saw in the stock market with regard to the housing crash occurred in early 2008 when it was fairly evident to many observers that housing was collapsing, that there were significant mortgage problems with the banks, and that the banks themselves would be threatened. Even given this information, the stock market continued to trade around 14,000. This made no sense to me. I saw no upside in companies' earnings, the economy, or the stock market, and the downside was that the stock market could very easily drop to 5,000 or 6,000. And yet the stock market continued to trade around 14,000 through most of 2008.

I still am not certain why this occurred. One line of reasoning is that almost all investment monies in the stock market are now handled by middlemen and agents who run mutual funds, hedge funds and other people's money. Possibly, these middlemen are more interested in their relative performance in the stock market than in actually earning you money. A principal would have pulled his money out of the stock market in early 2008, just because of the risks he saw that he might lose it. An agent, or middleman, running a fund may not care if money is lost because the money is not his, it belongs to his clients, and his motivation may be to stay in the market to be sure he doesn't miss some unexpected upturn and damage his performance relative to his peers.

This would explain why in recent history every time there was a slight uptick in the market, the market seemed to accelerate with buying interest, because these money managers were quite afraid of missing the next boom. It led to very increased volatility since the money managers had to jump in and out of every momentum play on the upside, and avoid downturns if their peers were selling. The smart move would have been to get completely out of the market during these tough times, but again, these money managers were being paid to invest fully in the stock market, so that was not really an option from their perspective.

I personally face quite a dilemma. In my heart I believe the stock market is very efficient and not only processes all publicly available relevant information about a stock, but also includes a great deal of nonpublic information. I believe there are major Wall Street players, especially hedge funds, that are trading on inside information.

At the same time, I am quite shocked to see that the market could be so easily fooled by the high-tech boom and the housing boom. If I'm right, it is another argument to get rid of middlemen and allow people to invest their own money themselves. Just as Milton Friedman was concerned about governments' spending of your money, I am concerned about middlemen like fund managers and hedge funds investing your money. They can promise you that they are looking out for your interests, but eventually it will be exposed that they were always looking out for their own interests, attracting more money to their funds.

Lie #31 You should invest in companies with monopoly positions.

Jim Cramer often says on his television program that he is looking for companies that have a monopoly position and hold monopoly power in their markets. He dismisses whether monopolies are good or bad for society by saying that he is only interested in making money for you, his listener. He knows that if firms can establish monopoly positions, they can charge whatever they want for their product or service and generate long-lasting healthy profit margins and cash flow with little competition.

So one of the most popular financial advisory shows on television is recommending we look for stocks that hold monopoly positions in their markets and invest in them. As a matter of fact, this is not so different from the advice Harvard Business School and other business school programs give their students. They suggest that the best-run companies and the most successful companies are those that establish monopoly-like positions. They preach that the less competition there is, the better, and the more dominating you are in your market the better. Many advise, like Jack Welch at GE did, that you control the number one or two market share in your business or get out of the business. And it is always smart, they say, to look for industries where market share is highly concentrated in two or three players.

The reasoning is quite simple. If market share of a particular industry is concentrated in two or three hands, you can very easily reach agreement with your one or two competitors to fix prices and to not compete on price. You don't have to have telephone meetings in the middle of the night with your competitors; you can very easily do your business through what marketing professors call price signaling in the marketplace. Simply, if one of your competitors decides to cut his price, you as the price leader and market share leader cut yours even more. It is a tit-for-tat game in which all competitors very quickly learn not to compete on price.

So successful financial advisors, and even our top business schools, are recommending that we look for companies to invest in that have monopoly positions. I find this absolutely nuts. Monopolies are illegal. There is a reason why monopolies are illegal. They avoid the traditional market mechanism of achieving profits by providing value to customers and instead achieve profits by overcharging their customers. If everybody operated as a monopoly, consumers, competitors and the economy would be much worse off.

So telling someone to invest in companies that hold monopoly positions is basically telling them to do something illegal, to profit by the illegal activities of others. It would be the same as saying: Why not invest in that company; they sell illegal drugs and make a great profit. It would be no different than saying: Invest in that company; they fence stolen goods and make a great return. Just because a company generates good cash flow does not make it a good investment.

Of course, you can always argue that the economy would not be materially worse off if you alone invested in these monopoly companies. But that is not fair. You have to ask the question: what if everyone did it? And given the fact that so many investment advisors and academics are recommending investing in monopoly companies, it's not crazy to think that everyone is doing it.

The answer is: if everyone invested in monopoly companies, monopoly companies would have no shortage of capital and would be encouraged to continue stealing from their consumers and bankrupting honest competitors, competitors who wish to compete with them in the market on product quality and price. By investing in monopoly companies, you are helping to destroy the free market system. You are rewarding companies that cheat and punishing companies that wish to play fairly and compete and provide you greater services at lower prices.

This is where free-market capitalism has its greatest problems. It is in this area of collective action where one individual is motivated by his own ability to profit, but if all individuals act the same, the entire system is threatened. Capitalism, with its individually acting, utility-maximizing independent agents, has no answer for this type of problem. We will see it throughout this text under a number of different guises, but it is a major reason why we have regulation of our capital markets, and why even profit-maximizing investors must continue to act ethically and obey the law.

Lie #32 Annual cash flow (EBITDA) is a much more reliable measure of a company's earning potential than net income.

When I worked on Wall Street for Goldman Sachs I was one of the original founding members of their leveraged buyout group. Leverage buyouts are nothing more than borrowing substantial amounts of monies against a company's own assets, dramatically shrinking the book equity of the firm and purchasing or buying the company in an acquisition, based mostly on debt.

One of the innovations that came out of the leveraged buyout market was that investors began to focus more on cash flow rather than net income in analyzing companies. Mostly, this was a good thing. Cash flow is defined as net income after you have added back interest and taxes paid and depreciation and amortization expense. Depreciation and amortization were added back because they were non-cash flow items; they were simply book accounting entries that had no cash flow impact. Taxes were added back to net income because very few corporations pay them, regardless of the statutory tax rate. Especially highly leveraged companies do not have to pay taxes because the interest they paid on the company's debt was fully tax-deductible. Interest is added back because we want to know the total cash flow generated from the company, regardless of how it capitalizes itself with debt versus equity.

But today, the practice of looking at earnings before interest taxes, and depreciation and amortization (EBITDA) as a measure of the sustainable cash flow of a business over time, has gone too far. It turns out that this measure of cash flow is not sustainable in the long term. The reason is that you have not allowed for any depreciation of the company's equipment and buildings. The very depreciation expense which you added back to net income to arrive at this definition of cash flow now cuts both ways, because you are assuming your buildings and equipment will never need replacement.

A proper economic analysis, if you are going to use this broad definition of cash flow, also has to include the negative cash flow that must be made when you purchase new buildings and new equipment. But the modern investor focusing on cash flow typically forgets to include these cash expenditures, and just applies a multiple to EBITDA. By looking solely at cash generated from the business, she or he is shortsightedly forgetting that a business must make investments over time in its infrastructure, its equipment, and its buildings necessary to continue to produce that cash flow in the future. Remember, a stock has no value unless the company pays dividends over time. And it takes a very long time for those dividend payments to reach a net present value equal to today's stock price. You cannot assume that the company's current cash flow extends forever without subtracting the necessary investments needed over time to maintain that cash flow. By utilizing a cash flow approach rather than a net income approach to valuation, and by forgetting to subtract the major capital investments needed, the investor overvalues what a company might be worth.

Lie #33 Companies selling addictive products, such as liquor and tobacco, make for good investments.

If you look back over the last thirty years, and look for one sector that has outperformed all others from a stock return perspective, you would be surprised as to who the winner is.

It isn't the health care industry. It isn't high-tech. It is addictive products. If you create a fund of addictive products, including tobacco companies, liquor distillers, and beer distributors, this fund would have had the greatest price appreciation over the last thirty years, increasing some tenfold in aggregate. No other industry sector comes close to this type of stock price performance.

If you think the caffeine in Coca-Cola and Pepsi is addictive, which it certainly is, and include these companies in the analysis, the performance is even better. I don't include them here because modest amounts of caffeine have not been found to be harmful to one's health.

So here we have an investment philosophy: buy addictive product company stocks. It appears to work well historically and there is no reason to think it won't work well in the future. You might think that such representative products as cigarettes face regulatory sanctions in the future, but judging from the past it is doubtful they will meaningfully harm sales. In the United States such regulations have done little to halt the spread of cigarette smoking, and any decline in the domestic market has been more than amply made up for by increased international sales. Tobacco companies are less interested in 300 million Americans smoking than they are in 1.3 billion Chinese, 1 billion Indians and hundreds of millions of Africans.

But do you really want to be the owner of a company that sells addictive products that kill people? I can forgive people who smoke and get lung cancer or drink and destroy their livers because the products are extremely addictive and humans' free will is not operating properly. But I can never forgive rational investors who choose to be owners of companies that sell these products. Their decision, while appearing to me to be irrational, is made with full cognizance of what they are doing.

We have not outlawed the sale of cigarettes and alcohol because we don't believe it would be effective in decreasing sales of the products, and secondly we like to believe that individuals should be given the maximum choice possible with regard to their economic alternatives. The addictive nature of these products does make you wonder if the consumer is in a position to make a rational choice. But just because these products are not illegal does not mean that you should own a company that produces them. It is inconceivable to me that someone would choose to work for or partially own a company that creates a product that intentionally harms its users.

This is a very good reason why simple stock market indexes are not the answer to a successful investing strategy. Indexes cannot make moral choices such as this. Indexes invest in all companies, regardless of how they make a profit. It is up to individuals to send signals to unethical companies that they will not agree to fund their operations. This can be accomplished by investing in individual stocks and avoiding these addictive product companies, or by investing in ethical indexes that exclude them.

This seems to me to be a major problem with indexing in general. Indexing, by definition, invests across a wide array of stocks, but does not investigate the financial stability and creditworthiness of the companies, or whether the company's product and services are something that we desire as a country. Basically, everyone gets funding. You could extend this argument beyond addictive products to weapons manufacturers. We can argue whether you should support a company that makes hunting rifles, but there is little argument that we should be funding or owning companies that make armor piercing bullets to kill policeman or plastic revolvers that terrorists sneak through airports, or even our largest weapons manufacturers that are in a constant race to figure out how to annihilate the population of the planet. We can call new weapons systems "peace makers," but within our hearts we know that greater investment dollars going to additional new research for ever bigger weapons systems can do nothing but destabilize the world.

So if you are inclined to buy a tobacco company's or beer distributor's stock because of the unusual profit opportunity, I would suggest that you might explore whether you are as addicted to its profits as its customers are to its products.

Lie #34 High inflation causes interest rates to peak and, because rates are higher, common stock P/E ratios become depressed.

Why do stock prices seem to depress during periods of high inflation? If stocks are nothing more than percentage ownerships of real companies with real assets, you would expect, during periods of high inflation, for these companies' assets and earnings to increase in value, thereby increasing the price of their stock.

But this is the opposite of what we see. Housing, historically, has been a very good hedge against inflation, and during periods of high inflation house prices in nominal terms rise. But stocks, on the other hand, have declined during periods of high inflation.

One academic paper that tried to explain this argued that investors were irrational because they appeared to be taking the real earnings of the company and discounting them at a nominal interest rate that included the higher rate of inflation, thus arriving at a lower stock price. This would be wrong. If your cash flow in a net present value problem is real, in that it ignores inflation, then the discount rate used to achieve a present value should also be real: it should ignore inflation. So, for example, if you're going to use real cash flows to determine a company's stock price, you should discount them at real interest rates of 2 or 3 percent plus a risk premium, not at 15 or 18 percent, which includes expected inflation during high inflation periods like the 1970s.

This academic paper by Modigliani is famous because it is one of the first to argue that investors are not rational. Over time, this belief gave rise to an entire school of economic theory called the behaviorists. They believe that human emotions in general are often irrational and impact the value men and women place on stocks and other assets in the marketplace. If this is true, it is a direct assault on efficient market theory, which says that investors are rational and that assets are properly priced. It also threatens the foundation of all free-market capitalism because if assets are mispriced, there is no efficient distribution of assets in the system. You cannot have irrational people making decisions in a supposedly rational capitalist system.

But I think Modigliani was wrong. I believe that when inflation is excessive, stock prices go down, but I do not believe it is because people are irrational and mistakenly are using a nominal interest rate rather than a real interest rate in arriving at the value of stocks and companies.

I believe investors are not only rational, but they are smarter than Modigliani. I believe what they realize is that during periods of high inflation, companies' earnings actually suffer in real terms. Companies earnings prospects go down during periods of high inflation. In other words, companies' earnings do not keep up with inflation.

I believe this occurs because during periods of high inflation more and more people find it difficult to qualify for the loans necessary to make big purchases. Both houses and cars typically require that the buyer take out a loan in order to make the purchase. We know from recent experience that in order to take out a mortgage to buy a home you have to qualify for the mortgage. Similarly, you have to be in good credit standing to qualify to buy a car with a loan or a lease.

While applying for a loan is typically done by comparing your income to the interest payments required under the loan, regardless of whether we are talking about a car or house, during periods of high inflation with high nominal interest rates, it is much more difficult for a home buyer or automobile purchaser to qualify for the loan because his or her current income is not very substantial relative to the high interest rates charged. What the car company or mortgage broker fails to take into account is that due to high inflation, the purchaser's salary or income will be increasing dramatically over time with inflation. But that doesn't enter the equation. The credit decision of whether to lend a person the money needed to buy the car or house is based solely on his first year's current earnings, and this typically prevents a number of highly qualified people from making these purchases. What this means to the total economy is that two of the largest industries in our country, housing and autos, will slow during periods of high inflation. This will send the general economy into a tailspin, as all companies' earnings will be impacted and all companies' cash flows and stock prices should decline.

This is what we see when we look at the data. Companies' earnings decline and company stock prices properly and rationally also decrease. Investors are not being irrational. But academics who study the phenomena have done a poor job explaining it.

Lie #35 The stock market's two-decade appreciation is primarily due to growth, innovation, the opening of new markets and good management.

Many economists viewed the stock market's appreciation over the last two decades as evidence that the economy was healthy and that the business environment was good. They believed that corporate earnings were increasing because corporations were well-managed, innovative, and utilizing new technologies to better provide high value products and services to their customers.

I think many of these economists would be surprised to realize that much of the stock market's appreciation over the last twenty years was due to the simple fact that labor saw its wages frozen during a period of increased worker productivity. Real wages for workers in America have not increased for some twenty-five years. This is an incredible statement given that America, until just recently, has been the world leader in capitalism, financial markets, technology, and production.

First I will explain why labor has not participated in these American boom years, and secondly I will show why this leads to a significantly higher stock market.

The two great forces driving the organization of labor in the last quarter century have been globalization and technological change. While technology has allowed productivity to increase dramatically over the last twenty-five years, it has reduced many common manufacturing tasks to the simple task of pressing a button. The skill has been taken out of many jobs on the assembly line. As such, there has been a great influx of unskilled workers who can do these very simple assembly-type jobs. Corporations use this great influx of unskilled workers to force wages down even though their productivity improved. One can argue about how much unskilled workers deserve in pay, but I can assure you, you would not want to trade places with them for any amount of money in the world. It doesn't seem right that as productivity exploded, workers' wages declined.

Even more offensive to labor than technology improvements are changes wrought by the globalization of commerce in the world. Corporations decided, with no input from workers and citizens, to open global markets and to shift their manufacturing to the lowest cost countries available. American workers were put in competition with their fellow workers in low-wage countries like Mexico, China, and Vietnam, and regardless of their skills, jobs moved to these low-wage countries. The low wages were not a result of the skill level of the people, but rather a result of the cost of living in each of these developing countries.

It wasn't just manufacturing jobs that moved to low-wage countries. The Internet allowed administrative jobs and professional jobs in fields such as radiology, architecture, and engineering to be outsourced to countries like India. Again, it wasn't that Indian engineers were better than American engineers; they were just cheaper. And the reason they were cheaper is not because Indians were harder-working or more productive, but because it cost one quarter of as much to live in India as it did to live in the United States, so wages did not need to be as high.

Even if manufacturing operations in the United States did not move overseas, the wages of the American workers in the States were put under great pressure. Companies could constantly threaten to relocate plants overseas and use that threat to demand wage giveaways and benefit reductions. This also put great pressure on union organizations as any company could pack up and move its operation overseas if its employees even suggested starting a union. Of course union shops were the first to be closed and exported abroad.

This meant that during a period of increasing prosperity, the opening of new global markets and increased worker productivity, workers' wages were stagnant in real terms. Imagine what this meant to the stock market. Stock prices are nothing more than the present value of a company's future earnings. Earnings of companies increase dramatically when wages stagnate or decline. This is because workers' wages are the primary expense line item in a company's income statement. Typically, as much as 60 to 70 percent of a company's total expenses is labor. Earnings would explode if you could grow revenues without increasing labor costs. If a company's wages could be reduced 15 percent over time this would double typical margins in the company and, all things being equal, you would expect the company stock price to double.

This is exactly what has happened over the last twenty-five years. The stock market has increased some $8 trillion over the period. About $5 trillion of this is a real increase in values; the remaining $3 trillion is just nominal increases due to inflation. But this $5 trillion real increase in shareholder value can be fully explained by a simple shifting of value from the workers to the owners of these companies. If workers' wages had shared in the productivity increases that occurred during this period, they would have garnered at least $5 trillion more in present value of their total compensation. What has happened is that workers saw their salaries and wages freeze and the value created went to the owners of the companies.

Now that the financial crisis has started, we realize that much of the growth in GDP and in the earnings of these companies historically was not real to begin with. It was based on massive consumption financed with government and personal borrowings. Add to this the fact that labor has not benefited at all during the last twenty-five years and we see that the economic miracle that has been the United States over the last twenty-five years is quite a depressing story. It looks like, after adjusting for inflation and allowing for the fact that labor has not participated in its growth, the stock market would be down, not up, over the period. The Reagan miracle, the Republican strategy of greater free markets and capitalism, has ended up making capitalists and company owners richer at the expense of workers. This is why all measures of the quality of life in America have not increased during this period. The facts are that average Americans and workers are no better off, and it shows in their health care plans, their life expectancy, their education levels, and their take-home pay.

Lie #36 Low P/E stocks are considered bargains because they sell cheap relative to earnings, especially if they are big-dividend payers.

Price-earnings ratios are used to compare various stocks on a standard measure. If one stock trades at $50 and another trades at $20, you cannot say the $50 stock is more expensive. You must see what earnings you will get for that $50. If the $50 stock has $5 of earnings-per-share and the $20 stock has $2 of earnings-per-share, they both have a P/E ratio of 10 and you can conclude that they are similarly priced.

Not all stock should trade at the same price to earnings multiple. Higher quality companies with better managements, better growth prospects and less risk will trade at a higher P/E than smaller, riskier companies with fewer growth prospects and poor managements.

Financial advisers often recommend low P/E stocks as a bargain. But just as a $2,000 used wreck of a car may not be a bargain when compared to a $14,000 used Toyota, a stock traded at a low P/E is not necessarily a good deal.

P/E ratios are snapshots of a current year's earnings, or, at best, next year's earnings, and say nothing about earnings growth in the future. You may very well agree to pay a high P/E for a stock that is watching its earnings grow rapidly over time. In three to five years, a rapidly growing stock may have its earnings double such that its P/E would halve over that time period.

Similarly, buying a poorly performing company in a declining industry is not a good idea, regardless of the P/E. The P/E may be calculated on last year's earnings and the future may bring fewer earnings and possible bankruptcy.

If you go in search of low P/E stocks, considering them bargains, you will populate your portfolio with many troubled companies. That is why they are trading cheap on a P/E basis. Just sorting stocks by P/E is not sufficient to identify real bargains. You must do a more thorough analysis of the company's prospects and its management to determine whether this particular company has a bright future and great growth prospects given the price you're paying for it.

Similarly, many market prognosticators today are recommending stocks with high dividend yields. Often these companies have very low growth prospects and are themselves very low P/E stocks. But if you just buy stocks based on their dividend yield, especially in difficult times like today, you will end up with a large number of stocks that are declining in value. The reason their dividend yield appears to be high relative to their current stock price is that the marketplace has determined that they don't expect that dividend to be maintained in the future.

If you buy a stock whose dividend yield is 6 percent per year, what happens when the company announces it is cutting its dividend in half? To maintain the same 6 percent dividend yield the company's stock price would have to decline by half. Most likely, the stock will decline even more than that because the cut in dividends signals to the marketplace that the company is in a real cash flow crisis. Whenever a company significantly reduces its dividend it is admitting that it is running out of money, possibly facing bankruptcy, and has no other sources of capital it can access. More sophisticated lenders and investors have declined the opportunity of supplying capital to such companies.

So be very careful when trying to buy value companies based on low P/Es or high dividend yields. Often, you are doing nothing more than buying someone else's trash.

CHAPTER 5

Bond Investing Lies

Lie #37 Fixed-coupon Treasury bonds are risk free.

Investors rush toward Treasury bonds during times of crisis because they believe them to be risk-free. At many business schools, treasury bonds are often used in teaching as a proxy for a rich, risk-free instrument.

Treasuries are not completely risk-free. They face bankruptcy risk just like any other bond. But in the case of Treasury bonds, it is the US government that must default or go bankrupt before you lose your investment. Historically, this has had such a low probability of happening that it was not given much credence. If you believe the risk of the US government claiming bankruptcy or defaulting on its debt is zero percent, then short-term Treasuries are indeed risk-free, but longer maturity Treasuries still have risk inherent in them.

As you might guess by now, I don't believe the risk of the United States defaulting on its debt is anywhere near zero percent. It certainly is not as big as 30 percent either, but it could be significant enough that you may not want to hold all your assets in US Treasury bonds.

The problem is that if you don't hold your assets in US Treasury bonds during crises, where are you going to put your money? It is the US government that guarantees commercial bank deposits and now money market funds. It's hard to imagine a deposit at a major commercial bank being safe if the US government is in such bad shape that it defaults on its debts.

You may decide to hold your money in a basket of currencies, as the dollar itself would collapse if the US treasury ever defaulted on its debts. You could then invest in other countries' government bonds. There are very few countries that would weather a global financial crisis better than the United States. But, given the significant amount of debt in the US, it wouldn't be wrong to try to find other countries that you think might survive.

Switzerland is often named as a very conservatively-run country, but they may face a crisis just like Iceland in that the banks headquartered there have total assets and liabilities that are multiples of the government's entire GDP in size. Japan has also traditionally been a conservatively-run country with very little inflation, but if China is going to suffer due to a crisis, so is Japan.

Even if you believe that the United States has zero risk of defaulting on its debts, there is a real risk in holding long-term fixed-rate US Treasuries. That risk is inflation. If inflation were reignited and your fixed-rate Treasury bonds returned a fixed coupon each year and a fixed amount of principal, by definition your investment would not keep up with inflation, and your purchasing power would deteriorate over time. General inflation caused by printing too much money would cause all prices to increase, would raise the cost of living because of that price increase, and yet you and your fixed-rate Treasury investments would not adjust. You would be stuck with the old coupon and returning the old principal back. I say old principal because getting back your total investment won't help you in a world of increasing prices. If you invest one hundred dollars today and there is 10 percent inflation for ten years, and then you get back your hundred dollars at the end of ten years, you will have lost more than two-thirds of your purchasing power.

The same is true for any long-term fixed-rate security, whether it be a corporate bond, a municipal bond, or a US government bond. What happens is that in any high inflation environment, people demand a higher interest rate from their securities. But you are locked in your fixed-rate. Therefore, what will happen in the marketplace is that your bond's market value will go down. People will reprice it downward until your fixed-rate coupon represents a good market return given that inflation has reignited.

You might say—and I have heard this from many bond salesmen in my career—that you don't have any intention of selling the bonds early, that you intend to hold them to maturity. First of all, situations change. You may not think you need these monies until maturity, but if some unforeseen circumstance happened and you had to cash out of the bond, you would receive a significantly lower price if inflation returned.

More importantly, even if you hold the bond to maturity, all you are going to get back is your original principal amount. If you invest $100 you'll get back $100. But $100 after ten years of significant inflation is not going to buy the same amount of goods the hundred dollars bought when you made your original investment. So in dollar denominated terms it looks like you're being made whole, but in terms of purchasing power and in the amount of goods and services you can buy, you have suffered a real loss.

Lie #38 Treasury Inflation-Protected Securities (TIPS) bonds are risk free because they adjust for inflation.

Finally we might seem to be getting closer to a real truth, but this statement is a bit misleading.

It is true that TIPS bonds do adjust for inflation in the future. If you buy TIPS bonds and inflation reignites, they will adjust your principal repayment and coupon by the amount of inflation, and so protect your purchasing power. But TIPS are not perfect. During periods of deflation, both the TIPS coupon and the principal amount are adjusted downward by the rate of deflation. If that deflation is caused by a general contraction in the supply of money and the cost of living is thus going down, not up, you still have reserved your purchasing power.

But I believe that during very tough economic times like those we face today, you can have deflation that represents real price declines of, on average, all assets. By holding TIPS rather than a traditional debt security, you will have missed the opportunity to enjoy these lower prices by preserving your full initial capital.

TIPS securities are also unique in one regard. During periods of deflation, TIPS bonds at maturity pay the higher of either the deflated amount of the principal or the par or face amount. This means that the investor gets an added bonus by investing in TIPS during deflationary periods. While his coupon is adjusted downward by the amount of the deflation, because he is able to recoup his full principal amount at par, he has a windfall of increased purchasing power during deflationary periods.

There is one caveat. Be careful that you do not buy older TIPS bonds in the secondary marketplace that have increased in value due to inflation. If you buy a TIPS bond in the marketplace that is already valued at $130, the government's offer to give you the higher of the par amount or the calculated amount will not help you in a deflationary period; the calculated amount will be greater than the par amount.

This is all very complicated, but let me summarize. I still love TIPS as an investment. They do really well during inflationary periods and they are the only instrument I know of, including gold, that does fine during periods of deflation. All other assets try to keep up with inflation, but only TIPS guarantee that you will receive whatever the actual inflation rate is in the future on your

investment. For this reason, TIPS are a very good safe haven in difficult times when you do not know if there is going to be deflation
or inflation.

Lie #39 Interest rates are set by the Federal Reserve.

You can be forgiven if you have come to believe that the Federal
Reserve sets interest rates for our country. You hear this almost
every day in the media. Even economists speak about where the
Federal Reserve will set interest rates this week.

As long as the United States is a capitalist free-market country,
the marketplace will set interest rates, not the government. This
means that there is an actively-traded market for money at every
duration you can think of, from overnight to more than thirty years.
It is this market of active buyers and sellers that determines where
the necessary interest rate is for the duration of any security.

Bond traders take many things into account when determining
interest rates. First of all they themselves do not choose an interest
rate. What they do is buy and sell debt securities knowing full well
that when the price they pay for debt securities goes up, market
interest rates have gone down. As stated earlier, a fixed-rate debt
security is a promissory note to pay you a constant rate of return,
so it will effectively decline in value if inflation reignites and
interest rates increase in the future, so bond prices go down when
interest rates go up.

Just through the act of buying and selling debt securities, interest
rates shift. And there is no one interest rate. Interest rates vary
depending on whether you are investing your money for one day,
one month, one year, or for thirty years. Of course the cumulative
interest you earn changes, and I am talking about the effect of com-
pound annual interest rates for each of these different maturity
instruments. Normally, longer-term investments require a higher

rate of return and a higher interest rate. Some of this increase in interest rates on longer-term maturity debt instruments is due to the fact that they are less liquid, but I believe the higher interest rate also reflects a risk premium due to the fact that inflation may reignite in the future, and as we said earlier, with a fixed income investment you are not protected against increased inflation.

It is true that the Federal Reserve sets an interest rate at which commercial banks can borrow from it. The Federal Reserve sets the Fed funds rate at which depository institutions to the Federal Reserve can move deposits. It is a very short-term overnight rate, but because the Federal Reserve is such a gorilla in this bond-trading game, it can have a dramatic impact on very short-term debt instruments, and this in turn can affect other markets' rates of interest.

It is less clear that the Federal Reserve can influence longer maturity interest rates. Just because the Federal Reserve lowers a very short-term interest rate does not mean that people will agree to make longer-term loans at a lower rate of interest. A higher long term interest rate may reflect people's belief that inflation is going to come back into the system, or a belief that short-term rates may go lower. If short-term rates are lower due to deflation, you would be wise to lock in a higher interest rate for a longer period of time as an investor by buying longer-term maturity debt instruments.

We have seen this phenomenon recently as the Federal Reserve tried to loosen money by lowering the federal funds interest rate to near zero percent. They were hoping that this would stimulate bank lending and that longer-term interest rates, especially long-term mortgage interest rates, would decline. While there has been some decline in long-term mortgage interest rates, it has not matched the decline in the Fed funds rate and now long rates appear to be trending upwards. People today view residential mortgage lending as much riskier than they have in the past and are demanding a much higher risk premium over time to make long-term mortgage loans. In addition, just because the banks have more overnight money with easier access from the Fed does not mean they are willing to extend themselves and make very long term mortgage loans. In the past, they have packaged these mortgage loans through a securitization process and sold them upstream to long-term investors. Because of the crisis, and because people no longer trust the rating agencies and the commercial banks, the securitization market is moribund. Even the banks don't want to position long-term mortgage debt on their balance sheet.

So the Federal Reserve does set a regulatory rate, which is a very short-term rate. But this rate does not necessarily influence longer term interest rates, which are the key to setting mortgage interest rates and other long-term corporate rates of interest. Therefore, the Federal Reserve is limited in what it can do from an interest-rate perspective to stimulate the economy. Now that the Fed funds rate is nearing zero percent, the Fed is clearly hamstrung as it can no longer offer additional reductions in the Fed funds interest rate.

Lie #40 Bonds are a good investment and should represent a substantial portion of a typical individual investor's portfolio.

Most financial advisors recommend that you hold a mixed portfolio of bonds, stocks, and alternative investments like real estate. The percentages change depending on whom you speak to, but in general most will recommend close to 45 percent bonds, 45 percent common stock, and 10 percent real estate. It is common for younger clients to be pushed into higher common stock ownership, while more elderly clients are pushed into a greater percentage of bonds in their portfolio. An often-quoted rule is that you should hold your age in bonds as a percentage of your total portfolio. If you are sixty-five, you should hold 65 percent bonds in your portfolio.

The reasoning behind this allocation scheme is that financial advisors generally believe bonds to be a safe form of investment. They know that bonds are less volatile than common stock, which makes sense because bonds are higher in the capital structure of a company than common stock. If a company suffers a cash flow loss in the future, its common stock owners could take an immediate hit, but before a bondholder realized a loss the entire company's future would have to be threatened with bankruptcy.

But a company does not have to go bankrupt for its bonds to lose money. All that has to happen is that there be an increased chance of bankruptcy, or a decrease in the market value of assets available for disposition in bankruptcy. These probabilities are assigned by the marketplace every day, and if a company's fortunes decline and they have some significant debt outstanding, the debt will begin to trade off at lower prices until someone in the debt marketplace thinks that the higher-yielding debt securities are a good buy.

But the reason I don't like fixed-income or fixed-rate debt instruments as an investment alternative to stocks is that I believe debt instruments have much of the downside risk of stocks with little of the upside. This is especially true in the world we live in today, where companies are very highly leveraged. We have seen in a recent downturn that stocks of certain companies have fallen 75 percent, and their bonds are also significantly off, sometimes in excess of 50 percent.

I believe the biggest risk to stock investing in the long term is inflation. We have seen that stocks do very poorly during periods of high inflation. Long bonds also do very poorly during periods of high inflation because their return is fixed and their price has to come down so that a new investor achieves an inflation-adjusted real return.

So, very simply stated, both bonds and stocks have significant downside risk if inflation comes back or a company's earnings prospects deteriorate significantly. But what if things improve?

What if the economy gets better and a company grows faster than expected? The bondholder has no upside. Regardless of how well the company is managed and how good its earnings prospects are, the bondholder simply gets his promised fixed rate of return. The common stock holder has a percentage ownership in the company, and so if the company's fortunes improve, the return to the common equity holder improves. Simply stated, the bondholder is just going to get his money back in good times while the common stock holder has a real upside as the company's earnings improve.

I believe many individual investors are fooled into making bond investments. I think when they hear that they are getting a fixed return they think of that as a positive because they may be retired and looking for a fixed amount of income each year that they can live on. What they fail to see is that they may be missing a better alternative in stocks, and they already face similar downside risk to their principal by holding bonds. They are fooled by the name "fixed-income securities" when in fact their investments are no such thing.

Additionally, current income debt securities, both floating-rate and fixed-rate, are taxable on an ordinary income basis for any interest they earn. The key to any successful investment strategy is to pay as few taxes as possible—and if you have to pay taxes, don't pay them this year but many years in the future, and not at ordinary income rates but at capital gains rates.

Even in picking stocks you should do a significant amount of tax planning, because there is no reason, if you are a current income taxpayer, to put your money in mutual funds that pay a significant amount of dividends each year and create ordinary income. You would want to weigh your investments more heavily toward those stocks that pay less dividends and those mutual funds that do little selling, so that capital gains are realized but not for a long time.

But if you are a current income taxpayer it makes little sense to hold debt instruments that are paying interest at ordinary income tax rates. You could just as easily create a portfolio of common stocks and over time slowly liquidate your portfolio at capital gains rates to garner the same type of annual return that a bond portfolio would yield. If investing in stocks sounds too risky to you, there are transactions you can make utilizing puts and calls that will effectively prevent you from incurring a large loss in the stock market. This type of insurance isn't free, but it is an easy way to get bond returns out of a stock portfolio and pay capital gains taxes in the future, rather than the ordinary income tax due on current coupon payments on bonds.

Lie #41 Tax-free municipal bonds are a good investment alternative for a tax-paying individual.

Municipal bonds pay interest each year that is not subject to federal income taxation. Investors mistakenly assume that municipal bonds are a better deal for them than ordinary taxable bonds because they won't have to pay tax on interest earned.

But markets are much smarter than that. Because interest paid on municipal bonds is tax-free, what happens is that rather than pre-tax yields being equivalent on muni bonds and taxable bonds, the after-tax yields become equivalent in the marketplace.

What you would expect to find is that two bonds, one a muni bond and one a taxable bond, both of the same risk level, should have the same after-tax yields. So a muni bond yielding 5 percent pre-tax also yields 5 percent after-tax. But a taxable corporate bond must yield close to 7 percent to have an effective after-tax yield of 5 percent.

Under more normal market conditions, there is no tax advantage in buying the municipal bond because the market has already taken into account the fact that its interest payments are tax-free. In other words, you would expect to find comparable bonds to be yielding a higher pre-tax rate in the taxable environment than in the municipal bond market.

If it ever becomes the case, as it is in the current financial crisis, that municipal bonds on a pre-tax basis are yielding as much as or more than taxable Treasury securities, a warning should sound. Brokers will push municipal bonds on you as a bargain because of their high yield. But there is a reason municipal bonds are yielding so much in today's environment.

Municipal bonds, historically very safe investments, today are very risky securities. The reason is that the underlying municipality, state, or special government entities that issued the bonds are all in a great deal of trouble in this crisis.

Many of these entities have invested their cash proceeds and their pension surpluses in equities and debt securities and alternative investments that have taken a substantial hit in this market decline. Second, many local governments are going to see a dramatic reduction in their tax revenues as state and local income tax revenues decline, as property tax revenues decline, as home appraisals decline and as local sales tax revenues decrease due to lower consumption. The states will also face greater expenditures as unemployment insurance payments increase.

That is not the worst part of the story. On the expense and liability side, many of these state and local governments have an exploding time bomb set to go off. Many of their employees have very generous retirement and health care plans and many of these plans allow for full retirement benefits after twenty to twenty-five years of service. Fifty-year-old firemen, policemen, sanitation workers and other municipal employees will retire and either go to the beach or take second jobs. But they will garner very generous pensions equal to 50 to 75 percent of their full pay and enjoy the benefit of their high quality, very expensive health care plans.

Because the baby boomer generation is just now beginning to retire, the major component of this retiree cost is just now beginning to be felt by state and local governments. Some have argued that the current crisis will delay retirement for many, but I am not so sure. I think the arithmetic is such for municipal workers that they will do better by retiring and taking their pension and then doing whatever it takes, including working off the books, in order to earn a higher income after retirement.

The sheer magnitude of this problem is quite incredible. There is a small city outside of San Diego that is already spending 70 percent of its budget on retiree expenses, and this was before the current financial crisis began.

The problem cannot be solved by raising taxes. State and local taxes have been raised tremendously over the last twenty years so that they now represent more actual dollars in taxes raised than the entire federal government. These local governments have gotten very fat during good times, have very little incentive to fire employees or reduce wages, and now in bad times are going to try to ask taxpayers to pay higher taxes. I don't think it will be effective. Some municipalities have already tried to raise the property tax appraisal amount on private residences, but the attempt was met with great resistance since everyone knows home prices have gone down across the country. In a recession, I doubt taxpayers would vote for increases in either local income taxes or local sales taxes.

States and municipalities do not have to report as frequently as publicly traded financial institutions like commercial banks do about their financial condition. So as of now this story has been fairly well hidden. But it will be a huge story in the future.

And the market already knows. Yields on many tax-free muni bonds are dramatically higher than risk-free treasury rates, even though they are tax-free. The market is anticipating major problems in the municipal market. The worst mistake you can make is to go yield shopping when buying municipal bonds. If you invest in the highest-yielding municipal securities you are guaranteed to have invested in the riskiest underlying state and local entities. That is why their bonds are yielding so much in the marketplace to begin with.

CHAPTER 6

Lies About Other Investments

Lie #42 Private equity firms create value by taking a long-term per-spective and growing the businesses they invest in.

Until very recently, private equity firms have enjoyed very good returns on their investments. By buying companies in the public market at a premium and taking them private they have been able to garner returns to their shareholders in excess of 20 percent per year.

The current financial crisis has dramatically lowered these returns to private equity firm investors. Many private equity firms are now experiencing decreases in the value of their portfolios, not increases. They will be slow to recognize these losses as they do not have to until they sell a portfolio company or take it public. It is the nature of the business that they take their more successful compa-nies public or harvest them through sales first, and leave the dregs, the problem companies, behind on their balance sheet to linger.

But private equity firms have been successful for so long that it bears examining how exactly they made all these profits over the years. It is doubly surprising because, as I said earlier, it should be very difficult to buy publicly traded stock at a premium and gen-erate an adequate return to a private investor. The reason is that the public stock has great liquidity, which you give up when you take the firm private. Thus a private investor demands a higher return for making a private investment than for investing in a publicly traded stock with good liquidity. All other things being equal, this means that the company should be valued less, not more, in a private transaction. If the cash flows from the company don't change, and a private investor demands a higher return, that must mean that the value of the company to him is less to generate the required return.

So how did the private equity firms do it? The answer is that they dramatically increased cash flows. The public market has been criticized for a long time for taking a very short-term approach to running their businesses in order to satisfy the quarterly earnings reports so thoroughly perused by Wall Street research analysts. Public companies supposedly run their business quarter to quarter. I know this isn't true. The whole idea of having a publicly traded stock value is that the stock price reflects all the future dividends paid by the company to its shareholders. There is no way a company could have a value equal to thirty-three to fifty times its current dividend if investors were only interested in this year's cash flow. No, public investors take a very long-term horizon approach when investing in the stock market, and actually give credit to dividends one hundred years in the future when performing a present value computation to arrive at the value of a common stock price.

It turns out private equity investors are very short-term thinkers. They are focused on cash flow this year because they have to pay back the enormous amounts of debt they put on the company this year and make real, large, and current interest payments on that debt. Private equity firms are not investors, they are cutters. They cut wages, they cut unions and employee benefits, they cut back on capital spending and required maintenance, they cut back on new investment and growth opportunities to solely maximize this year's cash flow. They are not concerned about the future because they know they will unload the company soon and the future will be somebody else's problem.

They are not operating geniuses. They simply, through financial manipulation, increase cash flow in the short term by harming the long-term prospects of the company as well as shifting value from workers to owners. The only value they create lies in their attempts to solve the issue of managements of publicly traded companies that are not being responsive to their shareholders. In an upside-down world, they come in and police managements who are running companies for their own benefit rather than for the benefit of shareholders, but private equity firms run the company for themselves rather than for the benefit of the public shareholders. In neither case do public shareholders benefit tremendously. Public shareholders may feel good about being taken out at a premium to the current stock price, but this premium is virtually illusionary because it is a premium to a value that has been established by a poorly-run, self-centered management team that has been raping the company for years for its own enrichment.

In a world of diversification in which investors have so many investments that they cannot effectively monitor them, private equity firms and hedge funds act as policing agents of bad managements. But these middlemen themselves are extremely greedy, and rather than creating value for public shareholders, they end up grabbing the value for themselves. The solution is not to have more unregulated private equity and hedge funds, but rather to have less diversification, as I spoke of previously, so that individual and institutional investors can keep track of what companies' managements are doing and be certain that they have the shareholders' best interest at heart.

Lie #43 Investing in stock options allows you a greater upside, with limited to no downside risk.

If you have ever heard the pitch by a salesman to get you into the options business, it goes something like this. You have all the upside of holding the common stock, but with only one-tenth of the investment and none of the downside. Oh, were this but true. By now, hopefully you would be suspicious of such a statement because you know that in economics there is no such thing as a free lunch. If such an opportunity really existed, everybody would own options and nobody would own common stock.

An option is nothing more than a contractual right either to take a stock from a seller in the future (a call) or to force a buyer of the stock to purchase it in the future (a put). If you are optimistic about the company's prospects, supposedly you would be interested in buying calls, and if you are pessimistic, you should buy puts.

At least that is the conventional wisdom. It turns out that puts and calls are valued through a fairly complex mathematical formula that is indifferent to the direction you think stock prices are going. The formula assigns greater value to stocks that are more volatile, but options, like good investors, realize that you cannot predict the direction of a market and so are indifferent to people's feelings about whether a stock is trending upward or downward.

It is true that you can enjoy the same upside from owning a common stock with much less investment by owning a call option. But, unlike with common stock, you don't control this upside forever, but only for the fixed term of the call option contract, which might be three months or six months. Once the call option contract expires you no longer have an interest in that company, unlike the common stock investor, who enjoys the upside of the company's stock forever.

It is also true that if you buy a call option it will cost you much less than buying the underlying common, maybe 90 to 95 percent less. But because of the dramatic increase in volatility, and because at maturity in three or six months the option either has to be in the money or else be worthless, you are at much greater risk of losing your entire investment. If $100 stock trades down to $90, a stock investor still has $90, whereas a call option investor at an exercise price of $100 would see his entire invest-ment evaporate.

This is one of the basic tenets of investing. You should demand a higher return based on how much of your investment is actually at risk. When you buy a call option that is currently out of the money, you know that in three or six months it is very likely that it will expire worthless. There's nothing wrong with this, but you'd better be getting a very good expected return if the company's for-tunes improve and the stock price increases. If call options expire worthless a majority of the time, then when you are right you'd better get a multiple of your investment in return. It isn't a wind-fall when a winning call strategy returns three to four times your investment: it is absolutely required, given that most of the time you are risking your entire investment and it is expiring worthless.

Successful options investing is based on some of the most com-plex mathematical formulas in finance. Even with the aid of these formulas, there is no magic advantage to utilizing options rather than buying underlying stocks. As a matter of fact, sophisticated financial players can create synthetic call option positions through a series of transactions in the common stock market and the US Treasury market. After adjusting for risk, there really is no differ-ence between investing in options and investing in underlying stocks. The returns on a risk adjusted basis are equivalent, because if they were not, an arbitrageur would step in and buy the inexpen-sive opportunity and sell the more expensive, and drive the overvalued security back down to a reasonable level. For unsophis-ticated individual investors, my advice is quite easy to implement: stay away from options trading.

You may want to buy puts against your current common stock position in order to limit your downside risk in the common. But I can assure you that as a small individual investor you will be paying a very high premium for this insurance, as the put option will be very expensive, as will the transaction costs to implement the trade. Better, if you feel there is a significant downside to one of your common stock positions, to trade the common stock or at least reduce the number of shares you own until you reach a level of comfort at which you can successfully weather a downturn.

Lie #44 Venture capital funds are a great way of riding the high-tech wave.

Venture capital funds are a very strange investment vehicle. They make investments in thousands of very small companies in the hopes that a handful will grow to be such large companies in the future that it will create a positive return for the entire portfolio. Many venture capital firms never find these diamonds in the rough and end up disbanding. The most successful venture capital firms can point to less than a handful of companies that have generated almost all the return for the company over time. They are very proud of their Yahoo and Google investments, which returned thousands of times their investment, but what they fail to tell you is that 99 percent of their investments don't work out.

It makes it impossible for investors to judge which of the venture capitalists are good at their business versus just lucky. If two venture capital firms each have 1,000 investments and one has seven investments that have exploded in value and is deemed a market leader, while the other has only two investments that have worked out and is deemed a market failure, who is to say whether this difference between them is due to brilliance or just dumb luck? The number of success stories relative to a thousand total different investments is so low in each case that to reward someone who has a 0.7 percent success ratio and to punish someone who has a 0.2 percent success ratio seems excessive.

Venture capitalists are the classic example of a middleman. They really try not to benefit anyone other than themselves. If you have a good high-tech idea that you think will make you a lot of money and you bring it to a venture capital firm for a small infusion of capital, they will most likely end up grabbing a controlling position in the company and will eventually end up owning as much as 80 to 90 percent of your company. Your status will very quickly go from founder and owner to paid employee.

Similarly, as an investor in an IPO of a venture capital portfolio company, you should not feel as if you and the venture capital firm are partners. In such a transaction, they are clearly across the table from you. They are trying to unload a company out of their portfolio because they no longer believe it is generating sufficient growth for them to hold, while you as an investor are buying the company.

It used to be argued that these IPOs still had significant growth prospects attached to them, but they didn't fit into the venture capital firm's long-term strategy. Today, many venture capital firms are making much longer-term investments and some are even doing leveraged buyouts, so if there is a company in their portfolio that is certain to grow at 40 to 50 percent per year, it would make more sense for them to hold the company in their portfolio. The real reason venture capital firms take companies public is because they have lost confidence in the company's future growth prospects. They believe that the risk of holding the company in their portfolio is not worth it.

We have spoken earlier about why many high-tech companies are overvalued in the marketplace. People assume that the company will be around for a long time, and thus assign a higher multiple to the company's earnings and dividends in establishing a stock price than the short-lived company deserves. But it is the very nature of the high-tech business that many of these high-tech companies quickly find their products and services have been made obsolete as they are replaced by a new high-tech company's offerings.

One of the biggest schemes that was uncovered during the high tech boom and collapse at the beginning of this century is that investment banks, anxious to do business with venture capitalists, were inflating the value of high-tech companies going public. The standard strategy was to place IPO shares of a high-tech company with the investment bank's best big institutional clients, who would see a run-up in demand for the shares and then over a period of one to six months would unload the shares to individual investors. By the time the hype was over and the shares' price returned to earth, the investment bank's biggest and best clients were out of the stock and Joe Sixpack was left holding the bag. I was always amazed after the high-tech boom was over that more individual investors did not form class action lawsuits and try to recover some of their losses from the investment banks for having been fooled by such schemes. I believe vanity got in the way, as these investors would rather lick their wounds and quietly go away then publicly admit that they had been taken for tens of millions of dollars in such scams.

Lie #45 Commodity prices are certain to drop further as demand evaporates in this global recession.

Commodities are a very difficult investment to properly analyze and to arrive at a conclusion as to whether they are overvalued or undervalued. Whatever commodity you can name, from lumber to oil to pork bellies, is studied by so many thousands of experts who are more knowledgeable than either you or me about their particular field that it makes little sense to try to compete with them by trading commodities.

In today's environment, even if you wish to trade commodities, there is a fundamental problem with determining whether they are overvalued or undervalued.

Commodities recently went through the roof in price, with oil approaching $150 a barrel. Given my negative outlook for the global economy, I did not think such prices were sustainable and I said so, telling investors to sell oil, lumber, copper and every other commodity except for gold. I saw that the global demand for these commodities was going to shrink enormously in a severe global recession and it made no sense that their prices had accelerated upward.

The price increase was so dramatic, especially with oil, that I came to believe that it was not a true market price, that somebody was trying to corner the market. The last person who tried to corner a commodities market was Bunky Hunt, who tried to buy all the silver in the world and drive up its price. The commodity markets are so large and liquid that it makes it almost impossible for anybody to corner the market in any one commodity, especially oil.

There were hedge funds out there that would have liked to try, but they did not have deep enough pockets. But the deepest pockets in the world—the oil producers themselves, like Saudi Arabia—had a very good reason for wanting to push oil prices higher. It is estimated that with oil at $150 a barrel, Saudi Arabia has close to $100 trillion of oil still in the ground. That is $100,000 billion of oil. Propping up the price of oil artificially, cornering the market and manipulating the market price in the futures market might cost someone as much as $1 billion a week in real losses as he overpaid for oil each day in these markets. But $1 billion a week or $50 billion a year is chump change to someone who has $100 trillion of oil in the ground. Fifty billion dollars a year is approximately 0.05 percent of $100 trillion, a very small price to pay to prop up the oil market.

Having said that, even manipulated markets are subject to economic forces. It turned out that the global economic crisis was much worse than people had anticipated, and the price of oil collapsed along with most other commodities.

Some may think that the prices of commodities declined too much and are therefore an investment opportunity, while others may want to sell short commodities in the futures market, believing that their price decline has not ended yet.

There is a problem in implementing either strategy in the commodities market. The problem is that the continuing global recession is going to hold down real demand for these commodities for the foreseeable future. So real prices of these commodities will stay low and possibly fall lower. But the nominal price, the price you see in the newspaper for these commodities, may actually head higher. The reason is that the governments of the world who have been spending trillions of dollars to bail out their financial institutions may have to start printing enormous amounts of currency, causing general inflation. If inflation takes off, these commodity prices, at least their nominally stated prices, are going to explode, denominated in the currencies of countries that are printing money.

So this is the definition of a bad investment. Based on the research, you have uncovered two countervailing influences: real commodities prices might go down because of the lack of real demand in a global recession, but they might go up in nominal terms because of the reemergence of inflation. Best to stay away from an investment in which the most powerful forces driving the underlying prices are moving in opposite directions. The exception is gold, which has always been a good hedge against inflation.

Lie #46 Ignoring current disruptions, housing is always a very good long-term investment.

As you are probably aware, I have written two books critical of the housing industry and I am very negative on its pricing outlook. In 2003, I suggested to my readers that they sell their homes and rent, or at least buy Fannie Mae puts as a hedge, and in 2006 I predicted that the country would see real price declines of 25 to 35 percent in housing and that some cities in California and Florida would see price declines in excess of 60 percent. You therefore might be surprised to hear me name housing as a good investment.

Once housing returns to more normal levels, I believe it will be a good investment. The first question is obvious: what is a more normal level, and when will we see a bottom? Housing is still significantly overvalued in many cities across the country. Buying is still much more expensive than renting, even after the tax deductions, and this disparity will grow in the future as rents will come down due to the recession.

Banks are less willing to lend to new homebuyers and are demanding bigger down payments with mortgages harder to come by. People are not going to spend millions of dollars for a home if they have to put down 15 to 20 percent down payments, and they aren't going to qualify for the loan if their mortgage payments are not allowed to be more than 30 to 35 percent of their income.

Prices are going to have to come down further because there are no bank funds available to pay high prices for homes. But even if banks were willing to extend money to home buyers to purchase homes, I don't believe there would be many people anxious to buy a home in today's environment. It isn't just that they understand that it is a risky decision with upside and downside. They have also concluded that it makes little sense to put such a large percentage of their net worth into residential real estate. It certainly messes up their diversification plans by making them so highly exposed to residential real estate. And, for smart investors, it is not a productive use of capital.

If you live in your own home, it's not an investment; it is consumption. You are foregoing the investment income which is the rental income you might have earned by renting out the property, and instead you're consuming it by living on the property. You cannot assume that house prices will increase so dramatically in the future that you will have a positive return from living in the house.

But probably twenty-four months from now there will be real estate investment opportunities available to smart investors. It is easy to know when a real estate investment makes sense from a business perspective. The rental income not only covers the mortgage payments, maintenance, and taxes, but it provides you a healthy return on your investment. No longer can you assume that increasing house prices will bail you out of properties with negative cash flow each month.

If you can find such properties once housing bottoms, I do believe they are good investments. The reason is that housing over the long term is a very good hedge against inflation. Unlike stocks whose cash flows suffer during periods of high inflation, housing is a real asset, like a commodity, that should go up dollar for dollar with general inflation. If prices settle at a level where you can earn a healthy current return from the rental stream and still enjoy an inflation hedge on your principal investment, this is the definition of a good investment.

Lie #47 Gold is a bad investment because it has few productive uses in industry.

It is correct that gold does not have many uses in industry. Surprisingly, this turns out to be an advantage, not a disadvantage, when thinking about investing in gold. People do not invest in gold for its productive capacity. Gold as an investment is utilized solely as a hedge against inflation. Here we are talking about general inflation in which the average price of all things increases because the government is printing money. If the government prints twice as much money, and all other things stay the same, prices have to double. It doesn't mean that people value goods more, they just have more dollars because the government is printing them. But if you have investments like fixed-rate bonds that do not protect against the possibility of the government printing more money and causing general inflation, this can be a very serious problem in your portfolio. Therefore investing in gold is a good opportunity to hedge against unexpected inflation.

Commodities should do well during periods of high inflation. But, as we have seen, other commodities like lumber, copper, steel, and oil are so important to the productive economy that they may suffer in price as the economy declines. Gold, because it has very few productive uses, should not decline, and recently has not declined as other commodity prices have fallen with the global recession.

So again, the only reason to invest in gold is as a hedge against inflation. The supply of gold in the world is relatively constant. The fact that gold has few productive uses in industry means that the demand for gold is very low relative to the world supply. Also, many of the banking reserve systems for countries of the world hold gold in their reserves, so the supply is also huge and relatively constant—qualities you want in a currency.

Over the last ten years there has been the beginnings of a movement for reserve banks around the world to hold less gold and more marketable securities like Treasuries. Treasuries, paying a fixed-rate interest each year, have a real appeal to countries that earn no current return by holding gold.

One would have to think that this movement toward holding US Treasuries by countries' banking reserve systems has slowed, if not stopped completely. Countries of the world in the current economic crisis have to understand that even countries as large as the United States now have bankruptcy risks associated with them and that they run a real risk by holding obligations of the US government or even the US dollar. And dollars are yielding close to zero interest.

Gold is currently better than even the US dollar because the supply of gold in the world is relatively fixed. Because there are few productive uses of gold, there are few mines generating new supply. More dollars can be printed overnight and can cause tremendous diminution in value to someone holding dollars; the supply of gold in the world cannot be inflated quickly. This is the reason gold is an attractive investment opportunity if you are concerned about the countries of the world inflating their currencies.

Lie #48 Preferred shares are a better investment than common because they get paid first in bankruptcy.

I have always thought that individuals who bought straight preferred shares in companies might be the dumbest investors in the world. They are told that the preferred is senior to the common stock of the company, and that in bankruptcy the preferred shareholders will be paid back first, before the common is paid.

But preferred investments are still equity investments. As such, in bankruptcy, they will most likely be completely wiped out before the debt investors take a significant haircut. It's hard to imagine a company in bankruptcy that wipes out its common equity investors and then stops and pays its preferred investors back whole. In most bankruptcies, bankruptcy lawyers draw a line through the common and then cross off the preferred and assume that neither has any value in bankruptcy.

But even if you did have a stronger position in bankruptcy by holding preferred versus common, it doesn't make sense for this to be the key input to your decision-making process when investing. While bankruptcy is a very serious condition for any company, the risk of occurrence is so small that it makes little sense to let it drive your investment philosophy. Ninety-nine percent of the time a company you invest in is not going to go bankrupt, at least in more normal times, so you shouldn't base your investment decisions on what happens only 1 percent of the time.

The real problem with preferred stocks is the company's intentions. A company that issues a preferred stock is basically saying that it is so highly leveraged that it can no longer issue debt. It is creating a preferred dividend stream that is very similar to, if not more expensive than, the interest expense from the debt on its books, but it is not getting a tax deduction for the preferred dividends like it would for interest on its debt.

Companies that issue preferred stock cannot issue additional debt, but to satisfy their debt investors they have to increase the equity base of their companies. Such companies should raise new equity. But investors should want to buy common equity in such situations so that if the company turns around, the new common investor shares in the upside.

Preferred investors have no economic upside. They have all the downside risk of the common equity investor, and most likely in bankruptcy will lose everything, but unlike the common stock investor they can never get more money than their principal investment out of the company.

Because preferred stocks are such a bad idea from the issuing company's perspective, they have to be a bad idea for the investor. Not only can companies in trouble not issue debt, thus pushing them to issue preferred, they also probably cannot issue common equity. The reason is that if their fortunes have declined over the years, their stock price may be trading at such a low price that any new issuance of common equity would significantly dilute the existing common shareholders.

So, the reason to stay away from preferred stocks is that any company that issues them is admitting that it has too much debt and doesn't want to issue more (or that it may be prevented from doing so) and that its common stock price has declined so far that it cannot handle the dilution of new common equity.

Convertible preferred equity is another story. A typical convertible preferred is 100 percent convertible into common equity of the company, but at a premium price for the current market price. Here you are indeed sharing in the potential upside of the company, so I have no objection to investing in convertible preferred.

But don't think that you are going to outsmart the market and get this equity option for free. There are tens of thousands of people on Wall Street who make their living analyzing companies' convertible preferreds and arbitraging the difference between what the convertible preferred returns are and what the underlying common equity trades for.

CHAPTER 7

Lies in Economics

Lie #49 Unemployment is currently 8.1 percent.

We are told that unemployment reached a low in the current cycle of 4.5 percent under the Bush administration, and that at the start of the Obama administration it hovered near 8.1 percent on its way to 9 or 10 percent if economist projections are correct.

I don't believe these numbers accurately reflect the degree of unemployment that currently exists in our country. I believe the actual number is closer to 25 percent unemployment. I believe one in four Americans of working age wish to be fully employed and are not.

This is such a startling difference that if I am right, it raises questions about the credibility of all government statistics we are given and raises the question of whether we are being misled by our government. The horses in *Animal Farm* were continually misled by government-supplied statistics from the pigs that showed they were doing poorly, and their response was always that they would bear down and work harder. *Animal Farm* was supposed to be about a socialist dictatorial regime, but the similarities to how our government reports economic data are scary.

The 8.1 percent unemployment figure that the government reports to us only includes those individuals that are actively seeking employment, according to the government. Even the government admits that the 8.1 percent official figure becomes 14.5 percent when you include others, such as part-time workers, who would work full time if job opportunities were available.

But I think this number dramatically understates the magnitude of the unemployment problem.

To look at it from a different perspective, let us examine what percentage of Americans are employed rather than unemployed. There are 310 million Americans, of whom approximately 80 million are children, too young to work.

That leaves 230 million Americans old enough to work, of whom some are so elderly that they may not be able to work or so comfortable in their savings that they have been able to retire. In addition, some of this 230 million are college students in school and some are disabled and unable to work. Others are in prison. A smaller and smaller number each year are housewives who make a conscious decision to work at home rather than in the marketplace. I say smaller and smaller because the number of women who have full-time jobs has increased from 31 percent to close to 65 percent over the last forty years.

But—and this is the key—there are only 134 million Americans fully employed today. As a percentage of the number of adult Americans, this is only 61 percent. Even allowing for the elderly (maybe 3 percent of adult Americans are over the age of sixty-five), the disabled (approximately 1 percent of working-age Americans), the prison population (approximately 2 percent), college students (approximately 3 percent), and housewives (approximately 5 percent), we still have 25 percent of working-age Americans who are unemployed. And this doesn't count those housewives, elderly people, students and disabled who would work if jobs were available. If I am right, close to 35 million adult Americans are underemployed right now.

Besides lying to the American public as to how many of their fellow Americans are working—which is a prime indicator of the health of the economy—lying about unemployment has a far greater impact. The unemployment figure is used by many economists as a key indicator of whether an economy is operating at full capacity. When reported unemployment gets below 5 percent, most economists are satisfied that the economy is operating at full capacity and that any other stimulus measures would simply cause inflation.

We shall see later in this chapter that full employment is not the cause of general inflation in an economy. But imagine how damaging it is to an economy if the government and its economic advisors believe that everything is going fine because reported unemployment is 5 percent or even 8 percent when the actual figure is closer to 20 or 25 percent. What results is a large number of unemployed people who are ignored by the system and who live in poverty with poor health care, little opportunity to emerge from poverty, and a government that doesn't even admit they exist.

In addition, these permanently underemployed or unemployed people have to find some way to feed their children and so they become members of the underground economy, the black market. Many end up in criminal enterprises, many involve themselves in the illegal drug trade, and a good number simply give up. Two million Americans are currently in prisons. You can be certain they are not included in the reported unemployment figures.

Unemployment in our economic system is even worse than this. This is because America has exported much of its manufacturing capabilities overseas. Manufacturing is highly cyclical, and in downturns it is natural to lay off workers in the manufacturing sector first. Part of the reason unemployment did not spike in this recession until much later in the cycle was that our manufacturing was being done in China. Americans were not being laid off, but Chinese workers were. Twenty million plus Chinese are currently unemployed. I am not saying that we have to be as concerned about a Chinese worker as we are about an American worker. But we need to be aware that our economic system and its collapse caused severe unemployment in the world even before it hit home.

Similarly, the first layoffs in this recession were in the home building, home painting, landscaping and home renovation businesses. These are industries that rely to a great degree on illegal immigrants for their supply of labor. Another reason unemployment did not spike early in this recession is that these illegal immigrants lost their jobs, but they were never on the books as having jobs to begin with. They have always been paid under the table. Many Mexicans living in the United States illegally are now headed back to Mexico because of the lack of job opportunities here. Unfortunately, they will not face much better prospects there, as Mexico's recession is even deeper than the US's.

Lie #50 The current reported declines in real GDP are overstated.

Some have argued that the recent declines in GDP are overstated and that the economy will quickly bounce back from the current recession.

If anything, the GDP declines are understated. GDP was going to decline in the middle of 2008, an election year, until George Bush passed a tax cut which temporarily propped up the third quarter of 2008 spending. GDP subsequently went negative in the third and fourth quarters of 2008, but now will be propped up in the middle of 2009 by Obama's stimulus plan.

I believe that GDP needs to contract back to a more sustainable level. It is impossible for the government to hold GDP up at a level that was only obtained through massive borrowing and spending by consumers, businesses and the federal government. To try to continue this is futile. It is just like housing prices, which reached unattainable levels through loose mortgage lending and now must settle at more reasonable price levels that everyone can afford. To try to hold the GDP or house prices at unsustainable levels will be a futile exercise that will waste trillions of dollars of scarce government resources.

GDP as reported is real GDP; it has been discounted by the supposed level of inflation or deflation measured by the consumer price index. The idea is to find out whether the actual number of units of production has increased, regardless of price. It is called real because normally general prices increase due to increases in the monetary supply. These price increases certainly are not real. They don't reflect any increased demand for goods. Rather, they just reflect more currency in the system.

In the current environment, where people are concerned about deflation, I am not so sure that price declines are not real. It appears to me, and this is just my opinion, that real prices are declining across the board. People have less demand for goods at the current price level. They don't want to consume million-dollar homes, they have no interest in $600 hotel rooms, they have given up on $4,000 vacations, and they lack the resources to buy many $30,000 pieces of Tiffany jewelry.

If the price declines we currently see in this deflationary environment are "real," meaning that they reflect less demand from the consumer for those goods and less perceived value for the consumer from those goods, then reported real GDP figures understate the magnitude of the size of the decline in the economy. When we say real GDP has declined 5 percent during a deflationary period where prices also declined 5 percent, we have not measured the true magnitude of loss of value to consumers of that economy. Consumers not only purchased 5 percent fewer units, they also paid 5 percent less for them because they didn't value the goods as highly. This suggests that the real value of GDP declined 10 percent in this example if you include real price declines, not 5 percent as stated by real GDP.

Economists would argue that the reason we are in a deflationary environment is because the money supply is contracting. I am not so sure. The Federal Reserve has done everything in its power to inject reams of dollars into the banking system. Banks are de-leveraging and consumers, finally, are beginning to save. But the amount of high-powered money—that is, currency plus bank reserves—in the system is increasing, not decreasing, so it is hard to argue that this is deflationary. I don't pretend to completely understand it, but I do believe that the price declines we are seeing reflect real lower valuations in people's appreciation of the goods and services being offered in the economy. If the savings rate is increasing, that is one indication that people are looking for lower prices before they begin consuming again.

The reason I feel comfortable saying this is that prices had reached astronomical levels on most everything. Cups of coffee were selling for six dollars, blue jeans for $300, sunglasses for $250, magazines that you threw away after an hour were selling for five dollars, people were paying hundreds of dollars per month for cell phones and cable TV, bottles of wine disappeared at $50 a bottle and champagne at $200 a bottle, and some bars and restaurants in New York did not allow you to sit at a table unless you spent thousands of dollars on bottles of booze brought to your table. Prices had reached unsustainable levels and they had to come down, regardless of what happened to the money supply.

Lie #51 Inflation is caused by an overheated economy with too little unemployment and greater wage demands by workers.

General inflation is caused by the government printing too much money. This is very easy to see when you understand that all things cannot go up in price unless there is more money, more currency out there.

I am amazed at how few economists and economic pundits understand this simple fact. Every day during the boom, we were confronted with expert financial commentary that said that we had best be careful, that unemployment was getting so low that we could end up bidding up the price of labor and causing inflation in the general economy.

It's funny: stocks are allowed to increase in price, housing is allowed to increase in price, any commodity you can think of is allowed to increase in price, but as soon as wages start to increase, alarm bells go off in Washington and the government cracks down with a tighter monetary policy in an attempt to constrain increases in workers' wages.

One of two things is going on, both of them bad. One: maybe economists really don't understand this issue, which is mind blowing in its simplicity. Two, and more disturbing: economists do understand what's going on, but don't object or even explain what they know, because they are part of a system that is organized to keep wages down in order to improve corporate profits, including bank profitability. We shall see later that the Federal Reserve is more concerned with the economic health of our banks than that of the American worker.

Please do not think that I am making any of this up. More than thirty times during his tenure, Alan Greenspan was asked to testify to Congress about the state of the economy. Almost without exception, he was asked whether inflation was a problem that the country should be concerned about, and without fail, he stated that no: even though worker productivity had risen, the average worker's wages after adjusting for general inflation had not grown. He believed that it was his job, every time workers showed any improvement in wages, to step in and crush it. Whose wages do Americans think he was talking about? He was talking about your wages. It was a blatant example of who our government representatives and officials really work for: the big corporations that pay excessive campaign contributions and lobbying fees.

Lie #52 The Federal Reserve works for average Americans and is concerned with keeping the economy growing and vibrant.

It turns out the Federal Reserve is not part of the government; it is independent, and as such does not work on behalf of American citizens. The Federal Reserve is controlled by the Federal Reserve Board. Only the chairman of the Federal Reserve Board is appointed by the president of the United States. The other members are appointed by the regional boards, which are fully controlled by the country's commercial banks.

Historically, most people have assumed that the Federal Reserve was working on their behalf. It really wasn't. It was working on the commercial banks' behalf. On most issues that involve increasing the stability of commercial banks, the public would be supportive of the Fed. But on some issues, the interests of the public and those of the commercial banking industry are diametrically opposed.

I always believed that the Federal Reserve took action when the economy was threatened and jobs were threatened. I now believe that this is not their motivation. I believe that they take action when their commercial banks are threatened.

The Federal Reserve loosens money as the country heads toward recession, not because it helps in job creation as it claims, but rather to help their commercial banks, which are facing significant loan losses. By lowering interest rates and loosening money, the Federal Reserve makes it easier for the banks to recover their equity base by borrowing short at low rates and lending long at higher rates.

The Federal Reserve is definitely not pro-labor. They fear even good economic conditions that call for increased employment. Their concern is that if there is full employment, workers may be able to bargain with management and receive wage increases, which the Federal Reserve views as inflationary.

The Federal Reserve also is not interested in labor attaining fair wages. Wages of labor are a big expense item for corporations, and if they increase, corporations report lower profitability and have more difficulty paying their debts, many of which are owed to the commercial banks the Federal Reserve reports to.

People wonder why Alan Greenspan did not blow the whistle on the housing and mortgage crisis sooner, or why he didn't raise interest rates sooner when he saw a bubble was developing. The answer is that the commercial banks the Federal Reserve Chairman reports to were doing quite well during the boom. They were reporting record profits. This was not something that Alan Greenspan wanted to turn off. Greenspan was getting reports from all over the nation that mortgage lending was out of control, that there was fraudulent activity in the mortgage sector that was pervasive, that the terms of mortgages were so aggressive that they could never be repaid. He still did nothing.

Some people are surprised that the commercial banks got caught in this financial crisis and ended up losing a significant amount of money. But the amount they lost has to be compared to the hundreds of billions of dollars of profits they realized over the last two decades through aggressive lending to the housing sector, construction loans, commercial real estate loans, junk-bond loans, bridge loans, and loans to hedge funds and private equity groups, not to mention the exorbitant fees charged consumers on student loans, car loans, and credit cards.

It may not have worked out exactly like the commercial banks planned, but the Federal Reserve gave them everything they wanted. Less regulation, less transparency, greater leverage at the banks, no restrictions on their derivative positions, and a green light to mix investment banking and commercial banking activities that led to the entire collapse of the securitization business.

When the Federal Reserve was created, people didn't want a group that controlled the money supply to report to a political group like Congress. On the surface this sounds like a logical explanation. But instead, they had the Federal Reserve report to commercial banks. It was a dagger through the heart of every American working man and woman.

Lie #53 Business cycles and recessions are necessary and normal to a well-functioning economy.

We have lived with recessions for so long that it's normal for us to think that they are unavoidable, that they are a normal part of the business cycle. No one has ever convincingly explained to me why a normal economy has to go through booms and busts with recessions and the occasional depression, causing great harm to its people.

The conventional wisdom says that it is the nature of human beings that in good times they become overconfident and think the good times will last forever, and as such overconsume, overproduce, and over-stimulate the economy, leading to the eventual downfall we call a recession.

I just don't believe the conventional wisdom.

I think the banks and the Federal Reserve, which is controlled by the banks, cause recessions. I think banks are so highly leveraged and are so poorly run that they frequently have serious loan losses that threaten the banks' solvency. This is not as hard to do as you might think if banks are leveraged 20 to 1. A bank leveraged 20 to 1 only needs to lose 5 percent of its assets through loan losses and it is insolvent.

Each new decade we are surprised at how the banks have found new ways to lose money. Sometimes it is commercial real estate loans, in which developers have borrowed billions of dollars from the bank with no money down. In the past, farmers have been given loans from the banks and encouraged to buy equipment, and then as soon as they did the banks reappraised their agricultural land downward in value and called in the loan. In the 1990s, banks lent to leveraged buyouts that put huge amounts of debt on companies with no means of repaying the loan. More recently, banks decided that it was prudent to lend homeowners money to buy overpriced homes, again with no money down.

Regardless of which sector of its lending portfolio gets into trouble, the commercial banks' reaction is the same. They pull back on all lending to protect their threatened equity base. I believe this pullback in commercial lending causes recessions, just as their aggressive lending during good times causes unsustainable booms.

The Federal Reserve, which, as we have seen, is controlled by the commercial banks, only makes matters worse. They do everything in their power to help their beloved commercial banks, lowering interest rates in recessions and flooding the market with money. These low interest rates are nothing more than a harbinger of boom periods and bubbles to come as assets quickly become overvalued. The loose money the Fed injects into the system creates future inflation, which is extremely damaging to the economy.

I believe we can eliminate almost all recessions, depressions and asset bubbles through one simple maneuver: restricting the amount of leverage available to banks. If banks were only allowed to be leveraged 8 to 1 instead of 20 or 30 to 1, then a lending problem in a particular sector of their portfolio would not threaten their entire equity capital and they would not necessarily have to pull back on all lending.

I would make one other change to our commercial banking system. I would prevent bank executives and managers from taking cash bonuses, restricted stock awards, or stock option grants out of the company during good years. I would have bank employees work for a salary and a commensurate bonus of about 20 percent of their salary, not the 2,000 percent we have seen recently. And if a bank has superstar performers that want additional compensation, I would grant them restricted stock that they would partially have to pay for and which they could not cash in for ten years. I would thus ensure that they have the same long-term incentive as the shareholders to maintain the bank as an ongoing enterprise and a vibrant growing business.

Finally, I think we need to re-think having commercial bank deposits guaranteed by the US government. This seems to create a moral hazard that pushes banks to do ever riskier things on an ever more leveraged basis with no resulting capital diminution. Right now depositors don't care how risky the bank acts because they knows it has a government guarantee for the full amount of their deposits.

Some would argue that this government guarantee of bank deposits creates a more stable system. I disagree. I would get rid of the government guarantee of deposits, but I would also put a strict limit on how big any one bank could become. No one bank would be big enough to threaten the entire financial system if it went bankrupt. Depositors would have to do what they always should have been doing: decide which banks have a credible history of safety and security before they deposit their money in the bank. And I would disband the regional boards of the Federal Reserve and have it report to the people, not the banks.

Lie #54 Big job growth in a country is an indication of a healthy, prosperous economy.

Of all the possible economic indicators cited to demonstrate that a country is healthy and has a vibrant economy, we often like to cite the number of new jobs created, especially during a new presidential administration.

Bill Clinton likes to remind us that 22 million new jobs were created during his administration, and George Bush would like to forget that less than 2 million new jobs were created over his eight-year term (and 4.0 million were lost in 2008 alone).

While I don't want to say anything that could be misconstrued as being supportive of any of George Bush's policies, especially his economic policies, I don't think the preceding comparison is completely fair.

It turns out that during the Bill Clinton administration, tens of millions of immigrants were allowed to enter the country, many of these illegally. In addition, many housewives had to work full-time as a result of the stagnation in wages. Couples realized they could not live on one breadwinner's salary. Finally, many retired elderly people went back to work as they found that they really couldn't afford to retire.

So the number of jobs increased in the country because more people were looking for jobs. It's not really a good indicator of how healthy the country was. Especially when you realize that the majority of the jobs created during the Clinton and Bush administrations were low-wage service jobs in fast food restaurants, or caring for the sick and elderly in the health care sector, or working low-level administrative jobs, or fighting wars for the government.

So we have found that most of the major indicators of how strong our country's economy is are completely misleading. Job growth does not capture the strength of the economy, unemployment statistics are fraudulently reported and the GDP seems to continually increase for all the wrong reasons. Do you feel like your government is lying to you yet?

Lie #55 Tax cuts cause economic growth.

If something is repeated enough times we'll believe it. For too long we have heard that tax cuts stimulate growth in the economy. Even more amazing, we have been led to believe that if you cut tax rates, tax revenues will increase. A USC economist, Art Laffer, has made a career off of this simple, but misguided premise.

There is no proof anywhere, and there is no academic study published, that shows that cutting taxes generates more tax revenue or creates growth. Supporters of the idea like to cite Ronald Reagan's administration as proof that when you cut individual tax rates, the economy takes off.

It is true that Ronald Reagan drastically cut the statutory tax rates, especially on the wealthy. The wealthy saw their statutory federal income tax rate decline from something north of 70 to 35 percent. But this cut was illusory; the wealthy were never paying 70 percent of their income to the government. Because the statutory rate was so high, the wealthy spent a great deal of time with tax lawyers and other tax advisers to find loopholes and tax havens, so most of them ended up paying very little to no tax.

Even if you believe that Reagan's tax cuts motivated people to work longer and harder, it is impossible to find causality between his tax cuts and the improvement in the economy during his administration.

It is my very strong belief that what set the stage for growth under Ronald Reagan's administration was his decision very early on to get Paul Volcker, the chairman of the Fed, to quit printing money. Because the country was running at an operating deficit at the time, this meant that Ronald Reagan would have to instruct his Treasury department to borrow the deficit each year. He ignored the cries of economists who argued that such government borrowing would crowd out private investment and stall the economy. I believe he got most of his good advice from Milton Friedman, and in this case he was absolutely right.

It turned out that the government borrowing money did not crowd out any private investment; there was plenty of investment for all. As a matter of fact, that is what interest rates do. Interest rates increase slightly, and this attracts all sorts of new investors and new savings from all over the world.

But the critical element of Reagan's plan was that he stopped the Federal Reserve from printing money. This meant that there was no new currency being introduced into the system each year, and as prices stabilized, inflation immediately came down. Once people realized that the government was going to get out of the business of printing money—once people honestly believed it—long-term interest rates came down. The prime rate was 21.5 percent when Reagan came into office and eventually came down as low as 5.5 percent. Mortgage interest rates under Reagan were at 16 percent and reached an all-time low of 4.5 percent under Bush II.

I don't believe these nominal interest rate declines were responsible for the boom in the economy under Reagan because real interest rates never changed. Rather, as we explained previously, I think inflation itself is devastating to an economy because it prevents individuals from entering into long-term contracts to buy houses and cars, typically an economy's largest industries.

So Reagan did indeed take action that caused the economy to improve. But I am almost certain that his tax cuts had nothing to do with it.

An even better test of whether tax cuts can stimulate an economy came under George W. Bush. In 2001 George W. Bush gave a tax cut of approximately $3.5 trillion dollars to the wealthiest Americans. They did what any reasonable rich person would do—they put the money in the bank. They didn't create new companies, create new jobs, or stimulate the economy. Whatever growth there was under Bush—which was miniscule—it was not real. It was due to government spending for expensive wars, a dramatic increase in government spending overall, much of it on private subcontractors from Halliburton and similar companies, and a huge increase in consumption financed with borrowings by individuals on their homes. All of this debt-financed consumption was artificial, and all the growth reported in GDP under Bush was unreal. It is now all being given back, and then some.

The idea that tax cuts could increase tax revenue is almost laughable. Bush, because of his tax cuts, took a $250 billion annual surplus he inherited from Bill Clinton and Bob Rubin and turned it into $1.2 trillion annual operating deficit, now quite possibly on its way to $2 trillion under Obama's stimulus plan.

I believe that many economists don't actually believe this nonsense about tax cuts stimulating growth and paying for themselves with increased government revenues, but I believe they are afraid to speak out because they know the wealthy, the powerful, and the country's biggest corporations are in favor of lower taxes.

The other phenomenon I see is that out of all the good economists in the world, one nitwit like Art Laffer came out with his silly theory about cutting taxes to increase tax revenues and was immediately presented on television and in the media as some sort of genius. It's not that his idea was better researched or his academic paper was better written than the thousands of others by economists around the world. He wasn't selected for his genius; he was selected because this silly theory gave cover to the wealthy and powerful to steal from those less well-off.

Lie #56 Greater country wealth, on average, brings greater happiness.

There are a few basic tenets that are the foundation of any capitalist society. One is that people are rational, that investors and consumers will act in their own best interests. Given a choice, they will choose lower-cost goods of equal quality to consume and higher-return investments with less risk.

Second, if all individuals and corporations act in their own best interest, a marketplace will develop that will generate superior results. It is through each agent in the marketplace acting in his own self-interest that values are maximized in the marketplace and society is the most well-off. We will come back to this assumption in our discussion of collective action problem-solving later in this text.

Third, economists presume that as a country gets wealthier, its citizens will be happier. This seems almost tautological. But in this book we have examined many lies that on the surface appear quite logical. I believe this one is similar.

It turns out that studies have been done on how happy different people are with their lives and how this correlates with how wealthy they are. The results seem to indicate that individual happiness does indeed increase as household incomes increase, up to a level of approximately $10,000 per year. This seems logical, since your first $10,000 of income is mostly going toward life-sustaining goods and alleviating the pains of not having enough food, shelter, clothing and health care for your family.

Beyond $10,000 of household income, something strange happens. It appears that with each increasing dollar of income, individuals become less happy.

If this is true, it violates one of the major assumptions behind capitalism and growth. Think what it means if the people of Argentina with an average income each year of $10,000 are happier than United States citizens with an average income of $60,000. It seems unbelievable, doesn't it?

Well, not if you have been to Argentina. Upon arriving in Argentina, you see what is holding back their economic development. They live in a corrupt society with a corrupt government and a corrupt president with a corrupt legal system and a corrupt justice department and corrupt policemen. It's very hard under such a system to build a business, protect your property rights, avoid fraudulent transactions, have contracts honored and avoid having to pay bribes to officials.

But what is also very evident upon visiting Argentina is that the people seem incredibly happy. I have done no scientific research on the subject, but I can tell you my first impressions. It appears that the people do not live to work but rather work to live. They don't work eighty-hour weeks at their jobs, and they certainly don't take job stress home with them. They fill their lives with almost daily social events, surrounded by family members and large groups of friends. Dinner tables in Argentine restaurants are mostly set for ten or twelve people as opposed to settings for one or two people in America. And you cannot fathom happiness until you attend an Argentine soccer match.

Contrast this with the present-day United States. Burger King increased its profitability in America by taking out its four-top tables and installing more two-top tables when they realized most of their customers came to dine in ones and twos. People seem absorbed in their work and motivated to get ahead. The wealthy don't know how much is enough. Everyone seems to be in a race for status, striving for the biggest house, the fastest car, or the best job. But in a status race, only one person ends up being happy—the person with the biggest house or the biggest car. The rest of us suffer the pains of permanently coming in last, or at best, second.

New economic studies are beginning to show that what motivates people is not absolute wealth, but relative wealth. If our genes are driving us toward increased competition with our peers for status, then it's no wonder we become unhappy as we work harder and harder and only find people who are doing better surrounding us.

Obviously, the Argentine model is not perfect. But America has a lot to learn from it. There's no question that as America has become more successful its people have become more insular and lonely. Look inside any car on the highway and you will most likely see it has one occupant, the driver. Even those Americans who have embraced their immediate families have become more insular as they have withdrawn to their wealthy enclaves and their big houses. The enclaves have security gates with guards and the houses might as well have moats around them for how much interaction there is between neighbors.

There is good news in all of this. If indeed human beings do not need hundreds of thousands of dollars to be happy, it means that we have the resources to take care of people less fortunate than ourselves. We can make dollar contributions to charities, of course.

But what I would like to see is successful Americans spending less time in their primary jobs and more of their free time dedicated to helping the poor, the sick, the elderly and the disenfranchised of the world. I believe finding fulfillment in this type of work will do more to make us happy than status-seeking.

Lie #57 Social Security is a program that cares for our elderly poor.

Social Security was a program created by Franklin Delano Roosevelt in order to care for our elderly poor. At the time, during the Great Depression, there were very few elderly Americans and they were almost all poor.

Today, thanks to modern medicine, the number of elderly is growing each day and almost equals the number of working Americans. In Roosevelt's day there were thirty workers for every one elderly retiree in the country, and today there are only two workers for every retiree. As the baby boom retires, this ratio will move even closer to parity.

But not all of the elderly today are poor. As a matter of fact, as an age group, Americans over sixty-five years old are the wealthiest age group in America. Households headed by people over sixty-five years old, on average, have net worths of approximately $275,000. Contrast this with young Americans, ages twenty to forty, who have more like $30,000 in net worth per household.

The wealth is not evenly distributed among the elderly. There are some that are very rich, others that have substantial savings and retirement incomes and others who have few savings and are living off of Social Security.

It is estimated that 50 percent of the elderly have incomes that put them in the poverty category. But I think this overstates the problem. It is not fair to measure the economic well-being of a retired person by the amount of income they have. Rather we should focus on how much wealth they have and whether these assets are sufficient to provide for them for the remainder of their lives.

To focus on incomes seems inappropriate because the life-cycle savings model of economics suggests that we are supposed to save while we are young and consume that wealth when we get older. As mentioned earlier in this text, the net assets of the elderly in this country are growing each year, not declining. Even if your income was zero, if you have substantial savings you could live quite well in retirement.

The definition of poverty also does not fit well with the elderly. Poverty levels are those below approximately $19,000 of income per year for a family of four. Seventy-five percent of elderly Americans have their houses fully paid for. Most households headed by an elderly person don't have four people, but only one or two. If, and I realize this is a big if, their medical expenses are covered by Medicare, then they don't face lots of other big expenses in their lives. I am not suggesting that it is easy, but if their housing and medical expenses are taken care of, an elderly person can live on Social Security payments.

No one wishes to talk about any reform to the Social Security system, even though it is bankrupt and the young Americans who are paying in will never see any benefits from it. The key to the reform of Social Security is to realize that many elderly Americans today are quite well-off from a net worth perspective, especially relative to the young people who are transferring their wealth to them through the system.

You could simply make Social Security means-tested, but I think that would punish elderly Americans who paid in thinking it was a retirement account and that they would eventually get the money back. Just because someone is rich in retirement does not mean you can violate social contracts with them.

I think a much better way to go is to continue to pay Social Security to all elderly people, but after their deaths, if they have substantial estates they wish to pass to survivors, the Social Security Administration could be allowed to claw back the last three to four years of payments. Because elderly people never know what their true medical costs, nursing home costs, or end-of-life costs will be, it is natural for them to end up saving more than they actually need for the remainder of their lives. But it doesn't make much sense for the Social Security payments to go to their heirs. That was never the intention of Social Security.

A clawback of Social Security benefits after death seems to me to be an ideal solution. It does not harm the elderly American while he is alive, it does not prevent him from adequately saving for end-of-life costs, and it solves the inequity of young Americans with little savings spending such an inordinate amount of their income on older Americans with substantial savings.

Lie #58 GDP needs to keep growing for America's economy to be healthy.

Economists, I think from birth, believe that a healthy economy is a growing economy. They believe that growth solves all problems.

In a developing country with an average income of $1,000 per year, the economist might be right. Government policy in these countries should be very pro-business and pro-growth, because with growth comes an alleviation of suffering from poverty and sickness, as well as the means to educate a populace.

But in a fully developed country like the United States, I don't see how you can claim that growth is always good. We have seen previously that simply increasing the average income above $10,000 does not necessarily bring greater happiness. You can argue that it is the American people's insatiable appetite for consumption and materialism that drives it to greater growth.

I don't see it that way. I see corporations as the prime driver of ever greater growth in our economy. We have said earlier that corporations are not persons and so should not participate in fundamental societal decisions like how much growth we find to be optimal. Corporations are unthinking and uncaring. They are only as smart as the by-laws you write for them. The way we have structured corporations in this capitalist society is that they only exist to increase shareholder value, and a prime way of increasing shareholder value is through greater growth.

So, we have a society whose government is overly controlled by corporations, and we know these corporations unthinkingly and uncaringly only want greater growth. Think of how upside-down this is. We create a virtual, unreal entity called a corporation, then we tell it through its by-laws to only care about growth, then we let it contribute to and lobby our government, and then we end up with a pro-growth government without any discussion among the citizenry. The Frankenstein's monster that we created to serve us, the corporation, now wants us to serve it. Of course, similar things could be said about another virtual entity we created called government.

Let's examine a hypothetical future in which there is one human being standing on every square meter of the planet, people have to purchase oxygen because CO_2 levels are extreme, and people wear six-inch-thick soles on the bottom of their shoes because the Earth is too hot to stand on.

In this future world in which global warming and the increased population are causing the planet's severe temperatures, you might want to cut back on growth. Well, I contend one thing. Corporations in that future world would disagree. They wouldn't think about the ill effects of growth; they would not weigh the quality of life for humans; they would not be concerned about the destruction of the planet. They would do what they have always done, and that is to try to maximize shareholder value by increasing growth. These future corporations would lean on the government and would support policies to spur even greater population growth, even greater industrial output and waste creation, even greater development, and would push citizens of the world toward ever greater consumption under the corporate model that more is better and even more in the future is best. So, our government should not take its lead from corporations in deciding whether growth is good.

But our economists are doing everything in their power in the current financial crisis to prevent even a minor diminution in GDP. They cannot imagine a world where a decrease in GDP is a good thing. In the current crisis, there is no question that the world would be better off with less leverage in the financial system, less growth in leveraged consumption and with the GDP allowed to contract to a more reasonable level. The fact that the Earth itself is screaming out for less growth as we examine problems of global warming, water shortages, the scarcity of fossil fuels and so on is completely lost on these economists.

Think about what this means. Economists are basically saying that if GDP contracted to 2003 levels, it would be a catastrophe. This makes no sense. The year 2003 wasn't a bad one economically for the United States. What would be wrong with going back for a time to a lower GDP environment with those levels of consumption and production? We could all take a 10 percent cut in pay and be there tomorrow. And our economy would be positioned to be much more stable and productive. Of course, we would need to restructure our banks and corporations and reduce their debt loads so they could survive a smaller GDP world.

Some smart economist needs to think about how a capitalist society can be organized under a zero growth society. Companies and their stockholders should be rewarded for improving efficiency and productivity, not for just increasing their customer base amidst an ever-growing world population. Maybe it can't be done. Maybe this is capitalism's fatal flaw. Maybe capitalism will unknowingly push us into greater and greater growth until we suffocate our economy and the planet.

Lie #59 Improved technology leads to increased productivity, which leads to a healthier and happier society.

Another basic tenet of economists is that technology growth is good because it leads to greater productivity. On the surface, it is difficult to argue with this statement. Medical advances should lead to longer, healthier lives. Computer technology advances should lead to better information and more fulfilling lives for citizens. More robotics should free up people for more human pursuits than working on assembly lines.

But we have seen a great advance in technology during the last hundred years. And I don't think it is true that humans are working any less. It appears that humans are working just as hard. Maybe some of the back-breaking work associated with clearing the land or tilling the soil has been alleviated, but people are still putting in lots of hours at work in what appears to be a competitive race to do better than their neighbors.

Very few people are saying: Enough is enough. I don't need any more luxury goods. I think I will only work twenty hours a week and spend more time with my family and on my passions, whatever those might be.

We see that because of technology and productivity enhancements, it only takes eleven man-hours to produce an automobile on an assembly line. Think of what this means. If there were a world where the only good produced and consumed was automobiles, every person on the planet could own 200 cars. To some car enthusiasts, like Jay Leno, this might sound like Nirvana. But the point I'm trying to make is that we may very quickly be becoming a society that is so productive that it must encourage consumption and materialism in order to create demand for all the products and services that improvements in technology are making possible.

It may not be that Americans are demanding all these cars and boats and houses. It may be that through productivity increases, technology is supplying them. What this leads to is great pressure from corporations and society to emphasize consumption and materialism. Such an emphasis, which we readily see in corporate advertising, has to lead to a more self-centered society in which people are measured by how much they have rather than on how much they give. You can also see, under such a consumption-based society, how entire poor continents on the planet could be ignored because their per capita spending is not sufficient to warrant attention from these global suppliers of goods and services.

Again, I don't want to leave the misimpression that I am against economic systems that are good at producing and achieving productivity enhancements and cost savings. But along with corporations' sole emphasis on growth, this is another reason why humans, through properly representative government, must keep an eye on corporations and the economy to assure that these economic agents are working on our behalf and not working against us. Just because we can produce a lot does not mean that we should consume a lot.

CHAPTER 8

Lies in Finance

Lie #60 Debt leverage is good because it increases shareholder equity returns.

Academics have gone back and forth over the years in trying to decide what the proper amount of debt leverage should be on a company. In a world with corporate taxes, it appears that maximizing debt leverage on a company minimizes the amount of tax the corporation pays because interest payments to bondholders are tax-deductible. In a world of both corporate taxes and personal taxes the appropriate amount of leverage becomes less clear.

But on Wall Street there is no question. Investment banks and commercial banks have dramatically increased their leverage over the last twenty years. The commercial banks even went so far as to approach Congress in 2004 to raise the regulatory limits on the amount of leverage they can attain from 10 to 1 to 40 to 1.

They didn't stop there. Since 1982, Wall Street has been adding leverage on almost every company they can find. Regardless of how stable and predictable a company's cash flows are, Wall Street wants to put more leverage on them. This created the leverage buyout boom and is the explanation for the large number of private equity firms, most of them just leverage buyout shops, that have grown up since.

But academics, in their analysis of the proper amount of

leverage for a firm, only looked at maximizing the value of that one firm. They failed to ask the question, again in the collective action context: what if everyone put high leverage on their firm? You can see that even if one firm's value were found to be maximized through increased leverage, it could not be good for the entire economic system if everyone did it, because leverage increases volatility and risk.

This is nowhere more true than in our banking system. Our banking system is critical for providing credit to all of our industries and supplying a safe haven for individuals who wish to deposit their savings. Of all industries, the last one you would like to see highly leveraged is banking. And yet that is exactly what the commercial banking industry did worldwide.

I am sure the bank shareholders enjoyed the higher returns on equity that resulted from higher leverage in the banking industry. But even shareholders at some point realized they were risking their capital by putting too much leverage on companies. It is not clear that managements shared this fear. Managements were mostly rewarded with cash bonuses from current earnings and stock options that had great upside if the company did well, but little to no downside if the company went bankrupt. Therefore, you would expect managements to want infinite leverage; it would increase the value of their upside option, and they are fairly indifferent on the downside. They might lose their jobs, but this would be only temporary. These executives could move from one bucket shop to the next with relative ease.

So here is a beautiful example of why government has to regulate the banking sector. Even if shareholders got better control of their boards of directors and the boards of directors got better control of their managements so as to properly align management interests with shareholder interests, the shareholders themselves would like to see their individual companies leverage more than what is good for the general economy.

This problem does not go away when you put a size restriction on banks so that they can't grow too big to fail. Even if you have lots of small banks with varying degrees of leverage, you would expect investors to head to the one that has the biggest return from the maximum leverage. No, the only way out of this is for the government to step in and put a ceiling on the amount of leverage a financial institution can utilize. That is why they are called collective action problems. Without regulation, a free rider would enrich himself, but damage the overall system.

There is one other option. One stakeholder group that would not like to see huge amounts of leverage on its bank is the bank's depositors. If we removed the deposit insurance provided by the US government from commercial bank deposits, than depositors would punish banks that were overly leveraged by pulling their deposits out and putting them in a less leveraged bank. If you don't believe that government can properly regulate companies, or if you believe that government does a poor job of enforcing its own regulations, this could be an attractive alternative. Depositors under such an uninsured system could insure themselves by spreading their deposits over a number of banks so as not to lose their entire net worth if one bank went bankrupt. It's a simple question, really: do you believe that the government or individuals are better at policing the institutions that hold the individuals' money? You might think that passing a simple rule or regulation eliminates the problem, but we have learned painfully in this crisis that rules and regulations can be obfuscated. If you made the system smaller and more responsive to individuals by limiting the government guarantee and the maximum size of banks, certainly you would have isolated cases of people losing some of their wealth as small banks went out of business, but you wouldn't have the massive failures across the entire system that we are seeing today.

Lie #61 CEO pay is deserved because it is determined in a highly competitive market.

A good friend of mine came to me a couple of years ago and asked me if I found anything wrong with the level of executive pay in the marketplace. I think I gave the wrong answer to him, so I would like to return to the question here.

At the time, I said that boards of directors approve all executive pay and boards of directors report to shareholders, so if an individual company wished to pay its CEO 1,000 times what a typical American worker makes, it didn't seem to me that anyone had any reason to interfere with that decision.

Even some American workers feel it is somewhat un-American to have the government put limits on how much a CEO can earn. In their defense—talk about being the Devil's advocate—some of the best CEOs, if they were not running publicly traded companies, could go to work running portfolio companies for private equity firms and earn tens of millions of dollars in incentive pay if they were successful in turning problem companies around.

But—and here is where my analysis was wrong—this isn't really a competitive marketplace for executive salaries. The board doesn't really report to the shareholders. To a great extent it is hand-picked by the chief executive himself, and it is composed of many of his close friends.

Boards of directors try to avoid conflict by having a smaller executive compensation committee, composed of outside directors, meet to discuss chief executive pay. But again these are mostly good friends of the chief executive. To disguise their insider dealing on pay, these executive committees hire outside consultants who specialize in levels of executive pay. But these executive pay consultants are nothing more than whores who go from company to company accumulating data on what the highest-paid executives make and then using that data to justify paying the next executive exorbitant amounts. They know why they are hired and they deliver by bringing in ridiculously high estimates of the market value of a chief executive.

Chief executives argue that they themselves create tremendous value for their shareholders. This may be true, but I have found that many company stocks increase in price simply through dumb luck as commodity prices decline, raw material costs or labor costs decline, or other things occur outside of the control of the CEO.

Even if CEOs were credited with creating tremendous value for shareholders, that does not mean that the CEO should garner a significant portion of that value. Under this logic, a brain surgeon who saved your life would own you, because you would be willing to give everything you had to take just one more breath. Brain surgeons are well-paid, but their pay has to do with the supply of brain surgeons, not just with the demand for their lifesaving services.

Similarly, a CEO may claim that he can create great value for shareholders, but it is more difficult to claim that he is the only person in the world who can do this. The fact that others can accomplish this means that his pay should be dependent on what it takes to find an equally qualified person in the marketplace. I can assure you that there would be a very long line of very capable people who would be willing to slave CEO hours for $20 million a year.

Lie #62 The biggest advantage of the corporate form is to limit investor liability.

The corporate form, as a separate legal entity, is recognized as one of the great innovations in economics. Most credit the ability of the corporation to limit investor liability as the major reason for its success and popularity. Individuals can make investments in companies and know full well that there is a firewall protecting them from creditors from coming after their personal assets. Their losses are limited to the amount of their investment.

This is extremely important and advantageous in creating an economic system that works. But the corporate form has other benefits that are not as widely discussed.

Before corporations, most businesses were run as family-owned private enterprises. It was difficult to raise long-term capital because people either didn't see a clear line of succession in management or were unimpressed with the thought of having the founders' sons and daughters running the business. The corporate form allowed the business to survive multiple generations by becoming an entity in and of itself, and separate from the family.

This meant that growth was unlimited for corporations as was the time frame in which they could accomplish that growth. The result is that corporations grew not just for ten or fifteen years, like a family-run company, but for a hundred years. The downside of this is that corporations have grown to be very large, powerful entities. I would argue that they are so powerful they now control our government through their campaign donations and lobbying. It's hard to imagine becoming more powerful than that. And thanks to the corporate form, they never reach obsolescence. They go on and on and on, forever.

Do large corporations use this power wisely? Not necessarily. As we have seen, thousands of shareholders can band together under a virtual legal entity called a corporation, and then negotiate wage rates with individual workers. Not the fairest way to set wage rates. Second, very large corporations are enormously powerful in their home cities and communities. They can pretty much dictate how they will interact with the community with regard to local taxes, community relations, and infrastructure demands. Third, corporations have been notorious for using their power to minimize spending money on environmental issues, consumer issues, safety issues, workplace environment issues, and so on.

I have a theory that one of the big benefits of the separate legal entity called the corporation is that it allows individuals in executive management to do unethical things that they would never do in their own good family name. Quite ethical individuals seem to be willing to do some rather unethical things if they are done in the name of a corporation rather than under their family name.

So what better way to obtain a license to behave unethically than to form a corporation, make yourself an employee of that corporation, and claim that your actions, while not good for the community, your fellow citizens, or the planet, are indeed good for your shareholders? I'm sure executives at weapons-manufacturing corporations justify their existence by claiming that their weapons are used to maintain the peace. I don't know how executives at tobacco companies rationalize their purpose in life.

Lie #63 Complex financial instruments are tailored to benefit both the issuer and the investor.

This is certainly what I heard when I worked as an investment banker on Wall Street. We were hiring more and more quantitative people with physics and math backgrounds and setting them loose to create more and more complex financial products.

The explanation I was given was that these very complex products satisfy niches in the market and were a beautiful fit between a specific investor's need to minimize risk and the issuer's ability to flexibly raise capital.

I don't believe that is the case anymore. I watched in the 1980s as Drexel Burnham and Mike Milken grew their junk bond business from a small Los Angeles operation to a global enterprise. Mike Milken paid himself $765 million in one year, back when that was unusual. One of the keys to the profitability of the junk bond business that they had created was that it was enormously complex and difficult to understand. Any issuer or investor that wanted to try to better understand the risks inherent in a junk bond investment, or even to get a price on a junk bond trade in the market-place, had to call Drexel Burnham. There was no publicly available market-clearing operation and no publicly available information on junk bond prices.

What this meant was that all the secondary trades of investors interested in selling their junk bond holdings had to come to Drexel, and most new issuers had to come to Drexel because only Drexel knew where the buyers were.

In addition, it meant that Drexel could charge exorbitant bid-ask spreads on junk bonds in the secondary market because they had little to no competition. Complexity worked to Drexel's advantage because it made each issue so specific and unique that there were no alternative investments.

Today, there are many products on Wall Street that are similarly enormously complex. Some of the most complex securities came out of the mortgage business and securitization. It's hard to believe that most mortgages just twenty-five years ago were thirty-year fixed-rate mortgages held by a bank until maturity.

Supposedly, to satisfy investor demand and better fit their risk profiles, mortgages were placed in pools and then chopped up every which way. They were layered in tranches with each level having a different rating and a different risk profile. There were long tails and short tails to invest in, and no one other than the mortgage trader at the investment bank really understood where the risk truly resided or how to value and price all the unique pieces created.

Just like Drexel's junk bond experience, what the mortgage brokers created was a mortgage product that was so complex that no issuer or investor could completely understand it, and so would be dependent on the investment bank for valuation and making markets in the securities.

And this is just what they got. One of the reasons why Hank Paulson's TARP plan failed is that he thought he could utilize a reverse auction and announce a price, and then all the mortgage securities outstanding in that class would come back to him from the banks. What he didn't realize is that every one of these mortgage securities and the mortgage pools underlying them were completely different. Some held long maturity mortgages, some held ARMS, some even held some credit cards and student loans in addition to mortgages. They were so heterogeneous that there was no way Paulson's idea of a reverse auction would ever work, and so he scrapped it before he even began and instead just gave away money to financial institutions he was close to.

This enormous increase in complexity of mortgage securities did little to help issuers or investors, but, just like Drexel, it substantially increased the profitability of the investment banks and commercial banks. The issuing bank on a unique mortgage security knew where the buyers were and who held the particular security, and it was difficult to make a market in that thinly traded unique complex security unless you were the issuing bank. Bid-ask spreads were very wide, reflecting this illiquidity, and it turned into a license to steal for the investment banks and commercial banks.

Lie #64 The vast majority of mergers create enormous synergy value to the buyer.

People think that because two publicly traded companies merge, there must be benefits to each of them. This simply isn't so. It is the nature of mergers on Wall Street that the buyer must pay a premium to the existing market price that goes to the selling company's shareholders. But it is difficult, if you are an efficient markets person, to explain how the buyer could afford to pay a premium. An efficient markets person believes that the seller's stock price before the merger offer is the right price for the company and designates the correct value for the entire enterprise.

Buyers try to argue that they are paying a premium for control and go out of their way to try to justify the high premium price paid by saying that there will be synergies from the merger. This is true when two banks merge because they can close branches that overlap and get rid of unnecessary duplications in management. But many companies buy firms that are not in their industry and sometimes not even in their country. Under these mergers, it is difficult to see where there would be much synergy.

Academic studies have shown that buyers of companies that pay a premium to the current market price for their acquisitions do indeed suffer, on average. Not only do their stock prices decline after the merger, it is very typical for a buyer's stock price to decline on the announcement of a merger. To me, it's another indication that companies are run for the benefit of executives, not shareholders. If shareholders were in control of these companies, how many times do you think that a chief executive could make an announcement of a merger, witness an immediate decline in the shareholder price, and keep his job the next day?

My experience on Wall Street suggests that managements and investment banks are driving the merger binge. Managements always want to run bigger companies. Their egos are rarely satisfied. And their hubris allows them to think that if they can run a turbine company well, they can run a television studio in Hollywood just as well. Investment banks just want to get paid—something that only happens if there is a deal, any deal.

CHAPTER 9

Lies About the Global Economy

Lie #65 Corporations pushed globalization to open new markets for their products.

It is generally believed that the reason corporations pushed for globalization was to open new markets for their products and services. Certainly the push for globalization came from corporations, as I don't remember any public hearings or town hall meetings held across the country to register the public's opinion about opening up the economy globally. Most of the decisions were done behind closed doors and you can be sure that corporate lobbyists drove the agenda.

I don't believe that corporations were solely interested in opening new markets. I believe they saw globalization as a way of overcoming restrictive government regulations. What better way to avoid government regulations than to become bigger than the government itself? No one country can effectively regulate international trade, as its laws aren't applicable beyond its own borders.

Corporations realized that there really was no global international regulator of commerce. They themselves created the WTO, which was nothing but an organization that represented their interests. The UN was certainly not going to get into the business of regulating international commerce. And when you think about it, it would be very difficult to create a governmental entity that could regulate international commerce.

The whole idea behind good governments is that they are democratic, in that they represent the interests of the people. I, for one, would not want to see an international body that tried to represent the interests of all 6 billion people on the planet. I have always felt that democracy works quite well in small towns and smaller countries, but its limits are pushed when it comes to countries the size of the United States, and especially when it comes to a country as big as India.

So even if we *could* have one world government, I would be strongly against it. I just don't think democracy works across such vast distances and cultures. People have to be intimately involved in their government and they have to believe that what their government does has a direct impact on lives. An attempt at world government would shatter both of those notions.

But through globalization, corporations have been able to get beyond single-country governments. And it has been very effective as a method of avoiding regulation. American environmental laws became meaningless when American car companies built plants in the maquiladoras along the Mexican border. Consumer laws, which had protected Americans for generations from dangerous products, became meaningless with the onslaught of lead-based toys from China and poisonous pharmaceuticals from Southeast Asia. Fifty years of union negotiations and labor law became moot when companies threatened to shift union jobs overseas and close entire factories and move them offshore. You can be certain that American companies opening factories in China did not have to worry about OSHA coming in and cracking down because of workplace safety issues.

The WTO, acting on behalf of the corporations, insisted that any trade agreements negotiated include the type of protections that corporations needed to do business in a country. Property rights, especially intellectual property rights, were always highly protected in any trade negotiation, as they were fundamental to a corporation doing business. Contract settlement, contract enforcement, and a reliable court system to handle both, was always a part of any agreement. Unfortunately, labor issues, environmental issues, safety issues, and consumer issues were never discussed.

It's really almost unbelievable that we opened up the entire world to global trade without understanding the ramifications and with no concern for what it meant to consumers and workers. Consumers and workers make up 99 percent of the humans on this planet. The fact that we wrote trade deals to benefit imaginary enti-ties called corporations and ended up harming many humans is something history will have to explain.

Lie #66 Vast natural resource wealth is the best predictor of how wealthy a country's citizens are.

If you didn't study economics, you might think that what makes a country wealthy is the amount of its natural resources. Certainly, Saudi Arabia would have to be considered wealthy because they have $100 trillion of oil in the ground.

But some of the most innovative academic papers in economics demonstrably prove that those countries of the world with the greatest natural resources have the lowest per capita incomes. It turns out that it is a curse in the modern world to have great natural resource wealth if you wish your country and its people to develop rapidly.

The best explanation for why this is true is that if countries have great natural resource wealth, a dictatorial government can grab those resources and fund itself. It doesn't need to raise taxes; it just needs to control the natural resources of the country. Because the government is not dependent on taxes, that means the government is not dependent on having a healthy economy that can be taxed. In other words, governments of countries with big natural resource wealth don't care if they have a healthy domestic economy or not.

And it shows. One of the best predictors of whether a country will become stagnant in a less developed state is whether that country is run by a dictator, and the best predictor of which countries have dictators is the presence of abundant natural resource wealth.

South Africa was able to run the same undemocratic apartheid regime for decades even though 90 percent of its citizens were black and impoverished. There was very little real economic activity for most of the citizens of South Africa. The ruling white class simply lived on the natural resource wealth of South Africa, which, as you know, includes gold, diamonds, and oil.

The Middle East sits on one of the greatest reserves of oil and gas in the world, and yet for the last forty years has done very little to develop its domestic economies apart from the oil and gas industry. Qatar almost ran out of oil, and because of that was very interested in figuring out how to grow its other industry sectors. Unfortunately, before the study could be completed, Qatar found the third-largest natural gas reserve in the world off its coast. It went back to being a country solely dependent on oil and gas production.

The African countries are rich in natural resources, and it is a curse. Colonizers grabbed the natural resources without settling in the countries and democratic institutions such as the rule of law and effective courts of law were slow to come to the continent of Africa. Even today, China is busy building railroads to the sites that hold the natural resource wealth of Africa, but is less interested in building roads for use by the general populace. In Latin America and Africa all roads lead to the sea. They were built by foreigners so they could extract natural resources and leave.

Over the last decade, Africa has begun to show some economic growth; in 2007 the continent reported 5 percent growth. But much of this growth was due to the dramatic increase in commodity prices driven by China's endless drive for greater infrastructure building. Now that China's exports have slowed and China has pulled back on its infrastructure investments, commodity prices have collapsed, and so, I believe, will growth in Africa.

A healthy economy is a broad-based economy in which everyone participates. Great natural resource wealth allows rulers of countries to prevent that natural economic development process from occurring and instead to live off of natural resources until they have exhausted them.

Lie #67 International trade has been proven to increase the wealth of nations.

This statement is cited so often that it functions more as a truism than a true statement. I know what you are thinking. Please don't tell me that this is a lie. My belief system will be shattered.

There have been hundreds of academic papers written about trade and the wealth of nations. Many claim in their narratives that trade is good for growth, though their own statistical analysis shows little evidence of that. Economists are so convinced by David Ricardo's elegant argument of the comparative advantages of international trade that they conclude that trade is helpful to wealth creation before they examine the evidence.

Many of the academic papers go to great lengths to study wealth across numerous countries to try to find correlations with the amount of trade the countries do. When no correlation is uncovered, the authors of the papers draw conclusions such as: there is nothing in this analysis that would prevent one from believing that trade benefits country wealth. That's like saying there's nothing in this academic paper that prevents one from believing that the moon is made of green cheese. I don't want to know what the paper doesn't say; I want to know if you found any correlations to prove your thesis that greater trade leads to greater country wealth.

In 2002, Dick Roll of UCLA's Anderson School and I cowrote an academic paper that was the first to show that democratic institutions and civil liberties and a free press were not only correlated with greater country wealth, but that they could be considered causal to that wealth. In a sidebar, buried on the thirty-fifth page of our paper, we decided to also test to see whether international trade was important in predicting a country's wealth. By wealth in this case we meant average real incomes per capita.

Imagine our surprise when we realized that the variable that measured the total amount of trade a country does became completely insignificant in explaining the variance in country wealth across countries of the world. This meant that the various degrees of international trade a country enters into have no statistical correlation with how wealthy the country is. We were able to come up with this conclusion because Dick understood how to properly separate the impact of a number of independent variables in the analysis that were themselves highly correlated. It turned out that trade openness, how open the country was to outside ideas, was significant in explaining differences in wealth. And that makes sense. If a country closes itself completely to new ideas then over time you would expect its economy to suffer. But the sheer level of trade made no difference in predicting country wealth.

The world has changed since the days of David Ricardo. China does not have to import or trade for Italian shoes if it likes the way they are made. China can hire an Italian shoe designer to come work for them in Beijing, have Italian shoe designs outsourced from Italy on the Internet, or have an Italian shoe company open a factory in China and train Chinese workers to make high-quality shoes. It's hard to think of any skill that is not exportable today. Trade is not completely obsolete; people do need access to raw materials and commodities, and as we have seen there is a great desire on behalf of international corporations to produce in low wage countries. But no one has ever demonstrated that international trade increases the wealth of the countries that partake in it.

Lie #68 Democratic reforms are bad for economic growth because the voting poor will organize and insist on income and wealth redistribution.

Economists have long believed that democratic reforms instituted in a country could lead to a weaker economic environment. They see greater democracy as a movement toward letting common folks in on the decision-making processes that most affect them. And they fear one group in particular: poor people.

In an argument that smells of elitism, these economists claim that if poor people are given political power, they will quickly use it to redistribute wealth through increased taxation on the rich, nationalization of industries, mandatory wage increases and welfare subsidies for the less advantaged.

Getting all people involved in government is the basis of democracy. It is why democracy works as a form of government, and it is why economists should not fear citizens' involvement in their government's decisions about the economy. Remember, these same citizens make economic votes every day when they decide where to spend their dollars.

The poor in the world get blamed for many things, which I find amusing since they have so little economic and political power. They are constantly cited as the cause of instability, government deficits, government debt and general malaise in society and the economy.

The truth is that powerful elites, mostly the wealthy and big corporations, currently run this world. They should accept congratulations on whatever successes they may have engineered, but they definitely must shoulder the blame for the problems we face. Anyone who doubts this statement needs to go to Davos, Switzerland, for their annual conference of the wealthy and powerful, where they decide what the world needs next.

Poor people may not have a great deal of money, but they are not stupid. The reason democracy works is because the world has found that no one can speak better about the welfare of a group than that group itself. Even if there were smarter, better-educated elites who wanted to speak for a disadvantaged group, typically their own self-interest would get in the way and they would fail to represent any group other than themselves.

It isn't true that if poor people were instantly given total power, they would take what doesn't belong to them. You have to give the poor more credit than this, although I must admit that there is something appealing about the idea. Poor people, like people everywhere, are more analytical and understanding than that. They realize that in an economic system there are going to be economic winners and losers, and they realize that concentrations of wealth can be helpful by forming pools of capital necessary for investment and job creation. The poor are not asking for your money; they are asking for a world with economic justice and equal opportunity where they can be given a chance to earn their own money.

I believe the poor are the best advocates for a healthy economic system because I believe a healthy economic system is based on the rule of law, proper regulation and the courts. And if society does not develop these institutions, then it can't inspire people to participate, since people have a very good sense of fairness and justice, whether they are poor or not.

I did most of my thinking on this subject when I was working with developing countries trying to figure out how they could grow faster in order to limit poverty. It is ironic, and quite sad, that the same conditions and circumstances I observed over those years in the developing world now very much apply to the United States.

The premise of my 2004 book, *Where America Went Wrong*, was that the United States was becoming more and more like a developing country. I meant this not just from an economic standpoint—the US was becoming more heavily indebted—but also from a governing perspective, as I believed that big corporations, through their lobbying and campaign contributions, had taken control of our government. I believed that the United States was becoming less democratic each day.

Our academic work predicted that the less democratic you are, the worse your economy will perform. I realized that this corporate control of our government was leading to unfair regulation or to deregulation that would be the seed of its own destruction. My 2003 and 2006 books predicting the housing crash tied the troubles in the housing and mortgage market back to corporate lobbying in Washington as the ultimate cause of the predicted debacle.

Democratic reforms—like kicking corporate lobbyists out of Washington and depending more on direct votes in referendums of the people, rather than on our corrupt representatives—are not bad for our country. They are good for our country, our democracy and, somewhat surprisingly, our economy. But—and this is the key—you have to learn to trust the people, all of the people. If poor people scare you, then you probably need to get out and meet more of them, because they are some of the loveliest, most generous, and warmest-hearted people you will meet in your life.

Lie #69 Capitalist countries enjoy greater prosperity, but pay for it with greater income inequality.

Whenever I hear someone credit capitalism with creating opportunity for greater prosperity and growth for a country, they immediately follow it with the statement: this prosperity comes with a greater inequality of incomes and wealth.

It turns out that this is completely untrue. I don't know where this fallacy first started, but I can guess.

Imagine a country when it first begins industrial development under capitalism. You can imagine the United States at the beginning of the twentieth century, or China or India today. What you see in each case are very wealthy capitalist entrepreneurs and very poor farmers and workers. You immediately come to the conclusion that capitalism increases disparities in income.

But that is not how I see it. What I think is happening is that a very poor agrarian society is being transformed into a much richer industrial society. After this transformation is complete, everyone will be wealthier. But transformation must be accomplished in steps. Under free-market capitalism, the biggest risk takers, who move to the cities and start companies and employ their fellow workers, become rich. It's as if a portion of the society is industrialized while the others are still farming. You can see this very clearly if you contrast the richness of Beijing with the poverty of the farmlands of China. It doesn't mean that vast inequalities will always be present, just that it takes a period of time before everyone in a society adapts to an industrialized economy.

So there may indeed be a temporary phase that capitalist systems go through during which inequality increases, but in the long run, the greater economic growth and prosperity that capitalism ultimately brings also reduces inequality. Dick Roll of UCLA's Anderson School wrote an academic paper with me in 2003 in which we prove this statistically. The poorest countries on the planet were mostly dictatorships, and it was these countries that had the greatest inequality of incomes. The wealthier countries were mostly liberal democratic capitalist societies, and they had much less income inequality in their societies.

Americans are very sensitive to this topic, because of all the developed countries, America has one of the most unequal societies. We have a lot of work to do if we are to make American society more egalitarian, like the societies of our developed-country peers.

Americans have witnessed a growth in inequality over the last twenty years that I highlighted in my 1999 book, *Slave Wages*. There has been economic growth and prosperity in America, but inequality increased. This seems to violate the basic tenet of my argument above, but actually, I don't think it does. Corporations were successful in eliminating country borders when it came to investment dollars, capital projects, and the international trade of goods and services. Therefore, if you are going to talk about societal inequality, I don't think it is fair to pinpoint America. I think you have to look at inequality around the world.

When you take the whole world into account, it is obvious that even though hundreds of billionaires have been created, inequality has declined dramatically. Something like 500 million people on the planet who used to live on less than two dollars a day have successfully worked their way out of poverty. Most of this progress happened in the developing world, predominantly in China and India. Of course if you look at the United States as an isolated case, its workers did worse and its owners did much better under globalization, so inequality within the United States increased. But as I said, globalization is a *global* economic force, and it is only right to measure inequality across the entire globe. If you do this, you'll see that, overall, inequality decreased in the last twenty years.

Capitalism has no morals; it is an unthinking force. It doesn't start off thinking that it wants to help poor people. Corporations go in search of the cheapest labor they can find. During the last twenty years, this has brought them to China, India, Vietnam, Indonesia and Mexico. And this is where the economic engine of growth allowed workers to work their way out of poverty. Just twenty years ago, Chinese workers used to earn a dollar a day. Now Chinese workers in automobile assembly plants earn $3 to $4 an hour. This is the magic of a free-market system. It doesn't intend to, but it helps the poorest among us first.

I am not suggesting that a poor industrial worker in China has an ideal life. I understand that he or she leads a life full of hardships. And I think the world would be better off if we could regulate her work environment so as to minimize child labor, improve working and living conditions, and make her workplace safer. But, even without these improvements, there is no question that capitalism has served China well by greatly reducing the numbers of its population living in poverty and wanting for food, shelter and medical aid.

Lie #70 The US financial crisis and ensuing recession will be tempered and moderated to a great degree by the diversified global economy led by China and India.

You have heard many financial experts over the last year argue that any recession in the United States caused by our housing and mortgage crisis will be short-lived because the international economy will help pull us out. Specifically, China and India are mentioned as powerful economic engines that will help to replace any lost global demand from the US.

There are two basic methods that economists utilize to measure the size of a country's economy. First, they account for all the goods and services produced in the country, measured in the local currency, then they convert it all to US dollars at the market exchange rate. Looking at it this way, you'll find that the size of the economy drastically underestimates the quality of life in that country. This is because it costs much less to live in these developing countries than it does to live in the developed world.

So economists came up with something called a PPP, or purchasing power parity method, for comparing different countries'

GDP. By this method, the GDP of China, approximately $1.5 trillion, is adjusted upward to something like $6 trillion, because economists have determined that you could live in China for approximately one quarter of what it costs to live in the United States. What they are saying is that China's GDP has the equivalent purchasing power of $6 trillion in the United States.

But if we are talking about China and India pulling the United States out of recession, we really don't care about the purchasing power of their GDP domestically in China and India. What we care about is the magnitude of their purchasing power in the States, buying goods from us and making investments here. For this measure it would be wrong to use PPP numbers as the measure of the size of the Chinese and Indian economies.

So according to some economists, China's economy of approximately $1.5 trillion and India's economy of approximately $1 trillion are expected to pull the United States and Europe's combined $33 trillion economy out of recession. On the surface you can see it makes no sense.

The problem is exacerbated by the fact that China's economy itself is highly dependent on exports to the United States and Europe, and those jobs in China that are not directly export-related rely to a great degree on spending from people whose jobs are export dependent.

This argument is called decoupling. The emerging market economies of the world have grown sufficiently large that they have their own strong domestic economies, so they decouple from the United States and European economies. If you want to convince yourself that there has been no decoupling, run a simple graphical comparison of the Dow Jones Industrial Average over the last twenty years representing the US economy versus a composite index of all the world's stock indices, excluding the Dow Jones. In this comparison of the US economy versus the world's, you will quickly see that the two graph lines plot exactly on top of each other; there is almost a perfect correlation between the two.

This is one of the reasons I am so negative on my forecasts for the US economy. It is obvious to me that China and India will not be helpful to us in pulling us out of recession. As a matter of fact, as China's exports slow and its own economy turns south, it will pull back dramatically on its big infrastructure spending, which will impact commodity prices in the world and cause much of Africa and parts of Latin America to turn recessionary.

Lie #71 The bigger our corporations and banks are, the better, as it makes them more efficient and stronger global competitors.

Our corporations and commercial banks have gotten bigger and bigger over the last few decades. This was not unintentional. Because of globalization, we felt that our companies had to be bigger in order to compete with large industrial enterprises from overseas.

We even adopted a Japanese style of management. You might recall that during the 1980s, Japan was considered an industrial juggernaut. They were making the best cars in the world and some of the best electronics in the world, and it was the fear of many Americans that they would eventually dominate all industrial production in the world.

Back then, many Americans read books about how we could better emulate Japan's success. On the factory floor it led to implementing just-in-time inventory and group assemblies. From an economic perspective, we began to apply Japan's organizational style to our government, banks and businesses.

The Japanese economic system is very much a top-down economic model in which the government's Ministry of Finance decides in what direction the country should go, then notifies the commercial banks, which inform the giant industrial companies, which implement the new policy direction. It appeared to many Americans back in the 1980s that this was a beautiful example of government cooperating with business, one that should be emulated here in the States.

Of course, what was lost in all of this was the importance of government standing independent from business and acting as a regulator of business, not as its partner. Just because there is conflict between business and government does not mean that the system is not working; as a matter of fact, it's a good indication that it is.

So the United States allowed corporations to get much closer to government, and in some ways to control the government. They also allowed US corporations and banks to grow much larger in size. They became global behemoths, the largest of which were bigger than many countries in the world in terms of economic muscle and revenues.

The mistake we made is now apparent to all. By allowing these companies to become so big, we allowed them to become too big to fail. In a modern game of extortion, these companies took greater and greater risks for greater returns to their managements and shareholders, then held up the government and the taxpayers when they got in trouble, saying: You have to bail us out or else we will cause massive unemployment and a deepening recession, if not a depression.

This is not what capitalism is all about. Just as entrepreneurs under a capitalist society have to be motivated to take risks and form new companies, capitalism also means that when companies go wrong, they have to be allowed to fail. This is the whole concept of creative destruction: out of bankruptcies emerge new healthy competitors, with better managements and better operating philosophies.

We as a country have still not addressed the issue of companies being too big to fail.

Lie #72 The European economic model of greater social support from government is a bankrupt ideology.

Sweden, Norway, Denmark, and France have been criticized recently for being too socialist and not free-market oriented enough. Their GDPs have grown at approximately half the rate of the United States over the last twenty years, in aggregate.

Among economists, this is enough of a damaging statistic to suggest that these countries have failed economies. The conclusion of many economists is that free-market capitalism cannot peacefully coexist with a liberal government intent on providing welfare to the poor, universal health care to its citizens, and adequate housing to all. It is one of the strongest arguments of the school of economists that believes that for free markets to operate, they must be totally unconstrained and unregulated with no government involvement at all. The idea is that there is something intellectually pure about the free market, something sacred about the equilibrium it reaches, and that any involvement from outsiders, especially government or labor, will distort this reality and cause either a less desirable equilibrium or a complete crash of the system.

That is not how I see the European experience. I see it as a natural evolution of capitalism in which countries, including the United States in the 1930s, realized that completely free-market capitalism, while productive, can be incredibly harsh on human beings. Because such a system is amoral, it treats human beings as if they were just another economic input to the productivity equation. What the United States in the 1930s—and more recently, Europe—developed were government regulations that tried to ensure that individuals and corporations in the free market would still see greater economic profits while the government provided a safety net for the elderly, the disadvantaged, and the poor. Development, while good, was not to be allowed to proceed willy-nilly, running over the backs of workers. Rather, it was to be a regulated process in which all humans would be treated with dignity.

And for decades, the systems appeared to work quite well. Because these countries were democracies, the citizens themselves were able to recognize when government regulation or taxation became too severe, and so would simply vote for fewer strictures on business.

Then globalization came along. There is nothing natural about what globalization did to the developing and advanced economies of the world. There was no equilibrium reached in a world where billions of people were unemployed and would work for starvation wages. There was nothing fair about putting the workers of the developed countries of the world in competition with the world's poorest.

Europe recognized this, and did not embrace globalization as quickly as the United States. Because of this, Europe's union membership was much more stable than the United States. Its society had a much greater equality of income and less poverty and unemployment than the United States. But its growth did suffer.

So the idea that the liberal democratic European model for the economy is a failure is not fair. No economic model can survive the introduction of billions of unemployed workers. There is no economic model for introducing billions of workers willing to work ten-hour days for $2 to $3. The failure of Europe's economy to manage this transition is not an indictment of the European economic model; rather, it is an indictment of the United States's method of proceeding with globalization with no concern for the welfare of workers in the developed world.

Globalization, as demostrated in competition between US workers and the low-wage workers of China and India, is a wake-up call to the world's workers that in the new high-tech, borderless world, education is the key. Without education, workers the world over will always be put into competition with low-wage workers from the developing world. And if America adopts serious education reform, it might be the silver lining of a very cloudy experience with globalization.

Lies About Hedge Funds and the Derivatives Market

Lie #73 The credit default swap (CDS) market reduces risk in the system by allowing investors to hedge their exposure to default risk, and therefore has made this current crisis much more bearable.

The credit default swap market is a relatively new market that has grown from $140 billion ten years ago to over $65 trillion today.

The stated purpose of the credit default swap market is to allow companies to hedge against their risk and their exposure to companies possibly going bankrupt. As explained previously, in the CDS marketplace I can enter into a contract with an insurance provider in which I pay premiums each month, but he insures against a particular company I hold in my portfolio going bankrupt.

Unfortunately, that is not how the credit default swap market is being utilized today. More than 75 percent of the marketplace is not used as a hedging tool to minimize risk, but as a speculative investment vehicle to increase risk. People are basically betting on which firms will go bankrupt, and other poorly capitalized firms are accepting insurance premiums paid to insure risks they could never afford to actually even cover.

As a direct result of the existence of this very large new marketplace, systemic risk has increased dramatically. There are numerous reasons, but the primary reason is that the biggest players in the

CDS market are all highly interconnected. If any one of them went bankrupt, there would be extremely large payments due under the credit default swap contracts, which might bankrupt the system. And if any of them went bankrupt, the other players in the marketplace would suffer enormous counterparty failure, as the defaulted firm would not be able to honor its contracts in the credit default swap market.

Because of this interconnectedness in the credit default swap market, almost all financial institutions, including many insurance companies as well as other companies in the market, are considered too big to fail. Regardless of the number of shareholders or the amount of debt investors each of them has, the fact that they are counterparty to so many transactions in the credit default swap market makes it impossible to allow them to fail. The failure of any one major counterparty in the credit default swap market would bring down the entire credit default swap market and many of its players. We are talking about some of the largest financial institutions in the world.

Once companies, especially financial institutions, become too big to fail or are considered too important to the credit default swap market to fail, we have a serious breach of what constitutes a free market. A free market must have a mechanism in which poorly run companies with unsuccessful operating strategies can be allowed to fail. Enormous moral hazard is created when not only equity investors but also debt investors of companies come to realize that they cannot lose, that there is no downside, that their firms cannot be allowed to go bankrupt so there is no risk of defaulting on their bonds.

This is the definition of moral hazard. Investors will stop weighing risk and pricing risk appropriately, knowing that they cannot fail. You can imagine how much risk will increase in companies' operating plans if their own investors are not concerned about the level of risk.

Diversification, in which investors try to share risks, seemed like a good idea when it was proposed. Earlier in this book I have spoken about some of the downsides of sharing risk through diversification. The credit default swap market exemplifies what can go wrong when risk is diversified too broadly. Investors falsely believe they can't possibly have a significant loss to their portfolio since they are so well diversified. But we have seen time and time again that systemic risk causes many variable investments and companies to all decline together. Certain risks are not diversifiable.

The interconnectedness of the credit default swap market creates an enormous domino chain in which one company's troubles become all companies' problems. Capitalist systems are already enormously interconnected, with companies acting as each other's investors, customers, and suppliers. It makes no sense for these companies to also share default risk among them.

The credit default swap market is also responsible for much of the financial crisis. Although the financial crisis began with mortgages, it accelerated with the credit crunch, when banks stopped lending, even to other banks. The reason they stopped lending was mostly due to the credit default swap market. No one knew which companies held which assets, and worse: no one knew, if a company did go bankrupt, who would be hurt in the credit default swap market from having insured it against bankruptcy.

The entire system avoided transparency, but even if it had been transparent it was so interconnected that there could not have been individual company failures. Capitalist institutions created what they thought was a new idea in the credit default swap market, but its collective sharing of risk goes against the whole idea of capitalism, which is to have individual companies compete, not to have them make contractual arrangements that cause them all to fail if one of them fails. This is not capitalism; it is more like a parody of socialism.

Hank Paulson's hands were tied because of the credit default swap market. He couldn't let any firm fail because its bankruptcy would trigger payments in the swap market, and if it were a counterparty, its bankruptcy would cause massive disruptions to counterparties. He had to bail out every company before creditors took a single dollar hit, or else credit default swap triggers would be met and payments would need to be made. This simple idea of cross-insuring default risk was the end of capitalism as we know it in the developed world.

There is no way to reform this very bad idea and make it work correctly. It is a direct threat to free-market capitalism, and as such it needs to be dismantled. Net positions should be calculated in the marketplace, and those of pure speculators should be zeroed out with no compensation. The government can decide how much truly hedged clients should recoup on their contracts. But the credit default swap market should be shut down permanently.

Lie #74 The derivatives market should be unregulated to achieve maximum liquidity.

The question of whether the derivatives market, and specifically the problematic credit default swap market, should be regulated was addressed in 1999. Led by Bob Rubin and Larry Summers, the Clinton administration was strongly against regulating it, and had the full support of a Republican Congress.

It's difficult to say whether they were motivated by their ideology or by their closeness to trading firms, who had enormous profits to make. We have already discussed the problem of government acting too closely in concert with industry, so let us ask whether regulation should have been enacted from a theoretical standpoint.

Anyone who has looked at the derivatives market quickly understands that counterparty risk is significant. When one sees how complex the spider web of interconnectivity is in the derivatives market, one cannot but come to the conclusion that losing a major counterparty would pose a risk to the entire system.

It is also difficult to believe that these individuals did not fully understand that the risk itself was not completely diversified. They had all lived through recent financial crises in which the shock of the initial event was quickly transferred broadly through the system. Thailand's problems and the Asian financial crisis in 1998 resulted in Russia defaulting on its debts.

More importantly, everyone understood what happened when Long-Term Capital Management got in trouble. It is estimated that this one company had over $1 trillion of exposure in the debt markets worldwide. Their collapse triggered a takeover organized by the Federal Reserve and the New York Fed in which six major investment banks and commercial banks in New York ended up taking over their positions. The reason the company was not allowed to fail was that it was the view of the regulators—and obviously of the banks that came in to save them—that if they failed they would trigger a landslide of additional failures.

And the reason that Long-Term Capital Management got in trouble was because all their positions moved against them at the same time, regardless of how diversified LTCM thought it was. It wasn't just the Russian bankruptcy that hurt them. All of their trades in all currencies and in all classes moved together against them. This is the definition of systemic risk.

People today say that we did not learn the lesson from Enron that regulation is necessary. But Long-Term Capital Management stands out as an even more glaring example of ignoring a major warning sign about exactly the type of problem that engulfed the markets in 2008.

Again, it was explained as a liquidity crisis. Everything eventually is a liquidity crisis because companies in trouble do run out of money, and you can solve any problem by throwing more money at it. But all you had to do to recognize the risks in the CDS market, a market that guaranteed against defaults, was ask the question: what if a number of very big players begin to default at the same time?

Given how Hank Paulson has bailed out almost everybody without their having to go into bankruptcy, it doesn't add up that the entire system was threatened solely by the Lehman Brothers default. This oversimplifies the problem. It wasn't just that participants in the credit default swap market had to make payments on those companies that went bankrupt. They also had to come up with more collateral for those trades that were going against them. As the yearly cost of insuring against a Morgan Stanley bankruptcy increased from $30,000 up to $800,000 [per $10 million of insurance], the firms that had offered this insurance had to come up with substantial new collateral to maintain their positions.

It was these margin calls that ended up causing the credit crisis. Just as margin calls on stock had caused the stock market crash of 1929, margin calls on debt securities and credit default swap positions caused the credit markets to freeze in 2008.

In addition to margin calls in the credit default swap market, many of the largest players, including Merrill Lynch, Goldman Sachs, and Morgan Stanley, were receiving margin calls on the collateral they had placed for their overnight repo loans. These mortgage securities, corporate securities, and other debt securities were declining in value in the marketplace, and their overnight lenders were asking for greater collateral to be posted.

The effect of not regulating the credit default swap market has been a disaster. Until recently, there was no central clearinghouse for trades. Transactions were treated as if they were simply two-party transactions between a willing buyer and a willing seller. The interconnectivity and the counterparty risk that threatened the entire system were totally ignored. Nobody knew what any other firm's total exposure was, and there was no netting of transactions so no one could determine who was properly hedged and who was not.

A firm like AIG was typically on the same side of all the transactions. They almost always acted as an insurer, guaranteeing against the default of corporate bonds. Thus, when corporations' probability of default increased, they lost hundreds of billions of dollars.

J.P. Morgan was a much bigger player in the credit default swap market. The fact that they have not had massive write-downs to date suggests that they did a much better job of matching their books. That is, they may have guaranteed one client that IBM debt would not go into default, while at the same time paying a second client an insurance premium in case IBM did so. Their net exposure to an IBM default was much closer to zero.

Of course today it seems inconceivable that a $65 trillion high risk market dealing with corporate default was completely unregulated. At the time, the head of the Commodities Future Trading Corporation tried to warn Greenspan and the Clinton administration that regulation was needed immediately. He was shot down by Greenspan and Rubin. They used the all-too-familiar argument that government regulation would impede efficient trading in the marketplace. The fact that free markets need to be regulated and the laws and rules of trading enforced was completely lost on them.

Lie #75 Individual companies benefit from the derivatives market because it smooths earnings and reduces volatility.

The derivatives market today is a $600 trillion market. Given that the entire global economy is only $60 trillion in size, this seems absurd. Until the arrival of the credit default swap market, you could argue that the risks inherent in this market were not really as large as the full $600 trillion. This $600 trillion amount is the notional amount of all derivatives contracts. It is not the actual cash flows that are at risk because of the contracts. For example, I may agree to pay you a floating rate of interest on a $1 billion notional amount derivatives contract, and if you pay me the market fixed-rate interest, the only cash that changes hands is the difference between the two. This may be less than $10 million per year, but the transaction is reported as a $1 billion notional amount transaction.

The credit default swap market is quite different. Here the full notional amount is at risk, because the full notional amount is due if there is a corporate bankruptcy. So I believe a $65 trillion credit default swap market has a great deal more risk in it than hundreds of trillions of dollars of simple interest rate and currency swaps.

Companies buy derivatives as a form of insurance to hedge their risks. When you think about it, the major reason companies are interested in hedging risk is to smooth their earnings stream. They want their earnings over time not only to grow, but to grow smoothly. The thought is that Wall Street will reward them by assigning a higher P/E multiple to their stock if their earnings stream going forward is smooth and predictable.

If successful, they will have created an earnings stream that looks as if it has very low volatility. But in actuality, the underlying cash flows of the business may be highly volatile. They are paying a premium to third-party middlemen to smooth out these earnings. In effect, they are using shareholder funds to mislead shareholders as to the underlying riskiness and volatility of the businesses they are in.

You can argue that hedging against currency risks or interest-rate shock or oil price shocks is good business. And if that is all we were talking about, the derivatives market would not be so controversial. Managements may be more motivated to hedge risks that might bankrupt an individual firm than shareholders who are diversified in their investments across a large number of firms. When a single firm goes bankrupt, the management team is unemployed. The shareholders meanwhile still have lots of other profitable investments. In other words, it is not clear to me that a well-diversified shareholder, if he was fully in charge of his investments in each company, would pay third-party derivative middlemen excessive fees just to make sure that a single company in his portfolio did not go bankrupt.

But the smoothing of earnings did not end with hedging risk against highly unusual events. AIG entered into contracts with a number of companies that simply stated that if the company's earnings for the next quarter came in lower than expected, AIG would make up the difference. This is nothing more than earnings manipulation, which is illegal. It ended up costing the CEO of AIG his job. But it was a huge business, and squeaky clean companies like Warren Buffett's Berkshire Hathaway were also involved.

Imagine a world where companies report earnings to their shareholders that have been so manipulated in the derivatives market as to appear smooth when their base operating businesses have cash flows that are extremely volatile. And also realize that there is no way you can read the annual report of a company and understand that company's derivatives exposure. This gets at the real problem. The derivatives market destroys transparency and prevents sophisticated investors from doing proper credit and investment analysis of individual companies.

The derivatives market decreases the transparency of individual reporting companies through two methods: it creates reported earnings that are smoother and less volatile than the company is actually experiencing in its cash flow, and it creates guarantees and other liabilities off–balance sheet, such that an investor cannot determine what a company's true exposure to risk is.

Imagine the difficulty if you wanted to invest in a financial stock today. How can you invest in J.P. Morgan when you don't know what their derivatives exposure is? You may come to the conclusion that Goldman Sachs is a risky company threatened with bankruptcy and that J.P. Morgan is a well-run company that faces a bright future. But J.P. Morgan may in fact be guaranteeing that Goldman Sachs will not go bankrupt, so, not knowing J.P. Morgan's derivatives exposure, you may mistakenly buy J.P. Morgan stock and end up owning the risk of Goldman Sachs going bankrupt.

The world is completely upside down. The credit default swap market and the derivatives market make fundamental stock analysis and credit analysis meaningless. No one knows who has guaranteed which companies' defaults and what risk exposures individual companies have because the companies have traded these risk exposures to each other in the derivatives market.

I cannot emphasize enough what a serious threat this is to our financial system. The entire capital market is based on the economic assumption that a rational individual can make rational judgments about where to invest his money by analyzing companies' assets and liabilities and their earnings and cash flow. If all of these numbers are being manipulated through the derivatives market, you might just as well throw darts at a stock page as do any serious economic analysis of a company's prospects.

I faced this dilemma in 2003 when I wrote my first book predicting the housing crash. I realized that Fannie Mae and Freddie Mac were highly leveraged and were poorly diversified, as their entire asset base was dedicated to residential mortgages.

But when I read Fannie Mae's and Freddie Mac's SEC reporting documents and their annual reports, I was unable to make any sense out of the companies' balance sheets and income statements. And the statements did very little to help me understand anything about their derivatives exposure, even though both of these companies were among the biggest players in the derivatives market.

I ended up concluding that the companies were in serious trouble, but told my readers that I could not measure the exact magnitude of their problems because their financial reports were unreadable. At the time, I thought that it was a unique problem, limited just to Fannie Mae and Freddie Mac. I now believe that it is the key to why the entire global financial system faces meltdown and why the credit markets of the world froze. The reason is that no one can do credit analysis or investing analysis of companies or banks because derivatives are distorting companies' earnings and liability exposures so much that fundamental analysis is meaningless.

To unfreeze the credit markets, I believe we have to do something about derivatives. I would shut down the credit default swap market. In addition, I would insist that companies accomplish a complete disclosure of all of their derivatives contracts so that an investor can understand what their exposure is to all the risks in the economy.

Lie #76 On average, hedge funds outperform the general market.

Before the financial crisis started, there was a general misconception that hedge funds outperformed the overall market on average. Now that hedge funds are seeing enormous withdrawals of capital by their investors and now that something like half the hedge funds in the world will face dissolution, people are beginning to understand the real risks hedge funds faced.

But you could have seen this coming before the financial crisis. While newspapers and magazines made great headlines reporting the extraordinary returns of the top-yielding hedge funds, a simple calculation of all hedge funds' values showed that their returns over the years had been declining.

Before their most recent financial crisis, hedge funds on average were still reporting a premium return relative to the stock market. But given the amount of leverage in the hedge funds, and given how risky some of their investments were and how undiversified these investments were, it is not fair to simply ask who had a higher return, the hedge fund or the stock market?

The correct question is: after adjusting for levels of risk, who had the greater return? Here, academic analysis has shown that hedge funds really did not outperform the market, especially after allowing for their substantial fees and profit sharing agreements.

The whole idea of investing in a hedge fund is that you are betting on a supposedly savvy investor who runs the fund to earn unusual returns called Alpha returns. These positive returns are uncorrelated with the general stock market. Anybody can create returns that are highly correlated with the stock market. These are known as Beta returns and there is really no economic value in them, because all you have to do to create more of them is leverage up a stock index.

What academics found when they studied hedge funds is that, in aggregate, hedge funds were not returning any Alpha return. The total return of hedge funds over the years was simply a leveraged Beta return. They really did nothing for you that investing in a combination of the stock market and bonds wouldn't do.

It begs the question: why were people willing to pay such enormous fees to hedge funds to create average returns that investors could very easily create themselves for free?

Sadly, once it was recognized that hedge funds were doing nothing special to create their returns, Wall Street invented hedge fund indices that were nothing more than synthetically created indices made to replicate the return of hedge funds. They were simply some combination of holding cash and bonds and shorting the stock market, but they were found to very closely track hedge fund returns over time. But by definition, because they were created by holding broad indexes, they could not have had any special Alpha returns. The good news is that they eliminated the big hedge fund fees. The bad news is that they were just another method of getting lots of Beta returns, something any investor can do on his own.

It was as if Wall Street investigated the hedge funds, found them to be a sham, and then created a product that replicated them. Knowing full well that these new hedge fund indices created no value for investors, Wall Street didn't care and marketed them aggressively.

Of course, the big misconception most investors have when they look at hedge fund performance is that they only see half of the hedge funds outperform the average. Unlike in Lake Wobegon, Garrison Keillor's idyllic home where all the children are above average, in the real world I think it is always true that half of the hedge funds have to perform above average. It was investors' folly to think that they could pick which hedge funds were going to perform above average in the future. There seems to be some correlation between historical performance and future performance, which I will address later in this chapter. But now that the financial crisis has hit, many of these supposed outperformers have been exposed as companies that were taking excessive risks, most likely in the derivatives market, which was poorly understood by investors.

Lie #77 Investing in a fund of funds is a great way to minimize your risk if you want hedge fund–type returns.

Possibly one of the biggest scams I have witnessed in my lifetime is the concept of funds of funds. The concept revolves around the fact that the hedge fund industry is very secretive and closed, such that a single investor would have difficulty analyzing the various hedge funds and their managers when looking to invest. The second part of the pitch of a fund of funds manager is that many investors, like pension funds, understand that single hedge funds can be very risky investments, so by investing in a fund of funds this can offer diversification across a number of hedge funds.

A fund of funds is nothing more than investing in a fund that holds other hedge funds. Given that you could go out and buy the individual hedge funds yourself, I don't see any real value added from this practice. In addition, you end up paying double fees, enormous up-front fees, and shares of the profits to the hedge funds, and then another set of up-front fees and sometimes shares of the profits to the fund of funds.

What the fund of funds manager promises you is that he can ascertain which hedge funds are going to do well in the future. Certainly, given the recent disastrous performance of many funds of funds, this was not true. It was just as difficult for the fund of funds managers to try to predict future returns of hedge funds based on their historically reported performance.

These funds of funds also promised diversification. But hedge funds, because they are highly leveraged, because most of them are big players in the derivatives market, and because all of them are subject to liquidity or credit crisis risk, ended up being much more correlated than people realized in these funds of funds, for much less diversification than they promised.

In many cases, funds of funds were nothing more than a method for unscrupulous fund managers like Bernie Madoff to receive investment monies without any disclosure. The people who raised billions for Madoff funds did it completely blindly, telling investors they were lucky to get in and that Madoff would not disclose detailed financial information to them. It made financial analysis more difficult because you were one step further away from the principal. It was a system that was based not on fundamental securities analysis and credit analysis, but rather on relationships, winks and nods. I have very little sympathy for people who lost money with Bernie Madoff and other funds of funds. They not only avoided serious financial analysis and relied too heavily on relationships, but I believe that in their hearts they knew that the promised returns could only be generated if Madoff were bending the rules somehow. More on that to follow.

Lie #78 Bernie Madoff found a surefire way to earn consistent, but not exorbitant, returns year in and year out.

In perfect hindsight, people are shocked that Bernie Madoff was able to create a $50 billion Ponzi scheme with no real assets. The fact that the regulators did not catch on is mind-blowing. Imagine how lax regulation has become: the SEC, after numerous complaints about Mr. Madoff's fund, still could not perform a simple investigation to see if he had any assets at all.

I think it is less shocking that investors put their money with Madoff. You see, the beauty of any Ponzi scheme is that it's not all based on trust; you actually earn a real return, but what you don't know is that those investment returns are not being paid by real returns on assets, but rather from new investor money coming into the fund.

But from your perspective it looks like you are generating nice returns on your money. Madoff was very smart in one regard. He didn't promise 35 percent plus returns. That would be difficult to maintain in a Ponzi scheme and investors would find it suspicious that he was able to consistently create them. Rather, what he offered his investors was a consistent, but much lower, return on their investments. He only promised 10 to 12 percent returns, but he actually delivered them every year. Regardless of what the underlying stock and bond market did, Madoff's fund always returned 10 to 12 percent.

A sophisticated investor should have realized that this perfectly consistent investment performance was just as suspicious as a fund that returned 35 percent per year. It is just as difficult to create perfectly consistent, zero volatility returns in an uncertain world as it is to create usually high returns.

The fact that Madoff investors didn't ask questions when they garnered their 10 percent returns in both good times and bad leads me to believe that the investors realized that Madoff was probably not doing everything completely legally. There were rumors that

Madoff was cheating his trading clients by investing before them in stocks that they wished to buy. Investors in his hedge fund probably heard these rumors and probably believed them because they were earning returns that were too good to believe—but this didn't stop them from investing with him. That is why I have little sympathy for people who lost money in Madoff funds. The fact that these investors kept their investment portfolios with Madoff and reinvested much of their earnings makes them co-conspirators, in my mind.

Good Ponzi schemes involve paying people such wonderful returns that they stop asking questions as to where the money is coming from. Accepting money and not asking where it came from is at the foundation of most criminal enterprises. People who participate in Ponzi schemes without asking how the returns were generated should not be pitied when their investments go bad.

Lie #79 Hedge funds should remain unregulated, because only sophisticated, knowledgeable investors can invest.

This is the great lie that allowed the creation of the hedge fund industry and allowed it to grow to trillions of dollars with no government oversight or regulation, no transparency, and no financial reporting.

The stated theory behind the lie was that because hedge fund investments were limited to very large institutions and very wealthy individuals that had very substantial net worth, typically in excess of $5 million, you did not need the hedge funds to be regulated and they did not need to report their financial results to the Securities and Exchange Commission. The rationale went that the reason for having a Securities and Exchange Commission was to prevent companies from ripping off small, unsophisticated investors who are incapable of doing their own thorough investment analysis. Because hedge funds were only open to big, sophisticated investors, there was no need for any formal reporting or disclosure by the hedge funds.

I wish it could be that simple. I wish the damage the hedge funds have caused and will cause in the future could be limited to just their very sophisticated and wealthy investors. But this is not the case.

Investors in hedge funds were indeed sophisticated financial players. They can make no claim that hedge funds lied to them, acted fraudulently, or failed to disclose risks. That was the game they invested in. They knew they were investing with no protections, and at a later time they could not come back and say that the hedge funds failed to properly disclose risks or acted fraudulently. It was a blind bet. The hedge funds made no commitment to them as to what their investment profile would be. Only in the case where a hedge fund was violating criminal law can I see an argument in which its own investors might have a chance of recouping some of their investment from the enormous fees the hedge fund managers took out of the fund. Short of this situation, I think these hedge fund investors are going to face substantial losses, but I feel no pity for them since that was the deal they struck with the Devil from the beginning.

But the damage done by hedge funds to the financial system is not limited just to the losses suffered by their sophisticated financial investors. The real reason that hedge funds should have been regulated from the start, should have been transparent and should have been forced to report financial information to the SEC on a regular basis is that hedge funds are some of the biggest players in our financial markets. I don't care about the hedge fund investors, but I certainly care about the other market participants who have to deal with the hedge funds on a daily basis.

Hedge funds have fought, from their very inception, any requirement that they be more transparent. They are the country's largest contributor to Congress and to presidential elections, and the quid pro quo of their financial contributions to our government is that there be no new regulations imposed on them.

Of course they argue that the reason they don't want to be more transparent is that they don't wish to give up their trade secrets as to how they create their enormous profits. Just as Kentucky Fried Chicken does not want people to uncover their secret recipe for fried chicken, so hedge funds tell you that if they had to disclose their positions on a regular basis, competitors could not only figure out how they were earning their excessive profits, but would copycat them in the marketplace and end up destroying the profit opportunity.

It's a nice argument; I just don't buy it. I think the reason that people fight transparency and want to avoid financial reporting is simple. I think most people that are afraid of shining a bright light on their activities do so because they are pursuing criminal activities. I believe that the hedge funds, almost all of them, are breaking the law in one regard or another.

The simplest way to break a law and generate excess returns for a hedge fund is to violate capital adequacy ratios. There are limits in certain marketplaces as to how much leverage companies can have in holding particular assets. Hedge funds can very easily manipulate these capital adequacy ratios because no one knows what their capital is or how it is employed.

This may sound like a technicality, but it leads to a tremendously leveraged hedge fund industry that no one can properly analyze. This leverage creates enormous risk to the financial system because it threatens not only the demise of the hedge funds, but the banks that lend to it. Bear Stearns, while it had a significant mortgage problem exposure, also was one of the biggest lenders to hedge funds, and it was this exposure that I believe finally bankrupted Bear Stearns.

Ivan Boesky, one of the most famous inside traders of the 1980s, made most of his money not just through insider trading, but through violating capital adequacy ratios. He made bets in which he had very little downside because he held highly leveraged positions. Unlike today, the regulators eventually caught Ivan Boesky because in the 1980s, funds still had to report their capital positions to the government.

The second way that hedge funds can generate consistent, usually profitable results is with insider trading. It is the nature of the hedge fund industry to be plugged in to all the major investment banks and commercial banks and trading floors. They have more "special" information available to them than anyone. And they are such big payers of fees to the investment and commercial banks that the investment and commercial banks have a real incentive to keep them happy by feeding them even more special inside information.

It would be shocking if these hedge funds, with so much inside information available to them, did not do some insider trading. The fact that the SEC has not prosecuted any of them is an indication of how lax regulation has become. But I don't think that insider trading in the hedge fund industry is limited to a few bad players. I think it is the basis of almost all their investment decisions. It is how I explain how these rogue traders, who were never really that brilliant to begin with, were able to report 35 and 40 percent returns each year.

These enormous returns year in and year out violate everything I know about how efficient markets are supposed to behave. You're not supposed to be able to beat the markets consistently, and certainly the same people are not supposed to beat them each year. I have never met anyone in my life who consistently beat the market, with the exception of three or four people I knew on Wall Street— and they did it through insider trading. They admitted, without giving me the details, that their investment philosophy was not to invest at all until they had some special information on future corporate events, and then they invested it all. They were not taking any risks. They were investing in sure things based on their inside information. Hedge funds could not generate the returns they are without doing the same thing.

For example, for years Harvard University reported dramatic percent increases in its endowment funds. They also were investing a significant portion of their assets in hedge funds. While some might think that Harvard's fund managers were smarter than everyone else, I never believed this. Now that the fund managers have left Harvard and opened their own independent funds on Wall Street with terrible performances, it appears that the key was not good fund management. Harvard is unique in that many of its graduates hold some of the most senior positions in government and finance in the world. It would be very easy for a fund manager at Harvard to connect with these people and receive special information that was not public in the marketplace. It may have been done rather innocently. But I believe that these important government, financial, and corporate executives found a way to make a meaningful contribution to their alma mater without having to actually write a check. Rather, they shared with Harvard's investment fund managers information that had not yet been made available to the public. By trading on this information Harvard could generate unusual profits. I have no evidence of any of this other than that Harvard consistently reported results that outperformed the market, which violates my understanding of efficient markets. The fact that Harvard did this every year for decades means that if the efficient market theory is correct, there is less than a 1 in 1,000 chance that Harvard did it honestly. In other words: if no one can outperform the market, and Harvard did by a substantial margin for decades, the probability that they did it without cheating is less than 1 in 1,000.

The third way that I believe hedge funds have cheated to generate excessive returns is through market and stock price manipulation. Many hedge funds, although themselves quite small relative to total trading volume on the exchanges, focus their attention on one or two stocks, and so can be a very meaningful percentage of the trading volume in those securities. If one individual or company represents a substantial percentage of the trading volume in any single security, it can easily manipulate the stock as it sees fit. This was the basis of the penny stock market in Denver in the 1980s, which was shut down by the SEC. Market manipulation is illegal. Again, I don't have any evidence or specific examples of this other than the unusual and highly improbable returns being generated by the hedge funds. Since there are no reporting requirements for hedge funds, it is impossible to gather real evidence.

Individuals and companies have complained that hedge funds were unduly influencing their stocks. Some were complaining that short sellers had sold their stocks without owning them. This is not my concern. I can understand how short sellers provide a real service to other investors in an overly optimistic buyers' market. No, my concern is that we don't have enough regulation and transparency of the hedge funds to determine how they are earning their profits and whether they are manipulating stock prices and other commodities and asset prices in order to achieve it.

Again, the real damage done by the hedge funds was not limited to their investors. Rather: I believe they stole enormous amounts of money in their trading activities from people who ended up buying securities from them and selling to them. And I think part of the problem with the current credit crisis is that people and institutions are finally wising up. They realize that the stock market, the commodities markets and other markets are not fair games and that not everybody is playing fairly with the same publicly available information. You can call this a lack of confidence, but it really isn't. It is a realization that the markets have become corrupted. Why would you ever buy or sell stocks in a market where the person you are dealing with on the other side has information that will not be available to you until tomorrow?

You wouldn't. So under this analysis, I believe that the hedge fund industry, through its non-transparent dealings, has severely crippled the global financial markets in the world. This collapse of the capital markets is the primary reason for the disastrous recession we are entering. And it is the primary reason why just spending government money on tax cuts and fiscal stimulus plans will not be successful in straightening out this recession. The real problems are much, much deeper.

CHAPTER II

Lies About Government
and Regulation

Lie #80 The current financial crisis was caused by too much government interference in the markets.

Adolf Hitler said that if you are going to lie, tell a big lie. This
whopper certainly qualifies.

Conservative talk radio and conservative cable news programs
have begun a desperate attempt to try to describe the current financial crisis as a problem with government, not with the free market
or with private enterprise. They are pulling out all the stops. And
they are certainly not letting the facts get in the way.

Each week they throw up a new trial balloon and see if it sticks,
to mix metaphors. During the presidential campaign they blamed
ACORN, even though ACORN provided mortgage advice to less
than 50,000 people in the country. Then they went after the Community Reinvestment Act (CRA), claiming that this government act
forced lending institutions to lend mortgage money to poor people,
that poor people should never have been buying homes, and that
they were the cause of the housing collapse. As I explained earlier,
all of this is untrue.

They have pretty much settled now on Fannie Mae and Freddie
Mac, calling them government-sponsored entities but admitting that
they were major lobbyists and campaign contributors to our Con-

gress. They would like you to believe that Fannie Mae and Freddie Mac are parts of the government, when in reality Fannie Mae and Freddie Mac are completely privately organized for-profit businesses. Fannie Mae and Freddie Mac did contribute to the crisis, just like every other major private sector financial institution contributed: by lobbying Congress for less regulation, by over-leveraging their balance sheets, and by making loans they never should have, all to enrich their management and stockholders. But as I have said, there is nothing uniquely government-oriented about Fannie Mae and Freddie Mac. They did enjoy an implied government guarantee, which Hank Paulson decided on his own to honor, thereby making China and the rest of the world's investors whole on their investment in the bankrupt Fannie Mae and Freddie Mac.

Of course the government did have a very large role in this crisis. But I believe that the free-market crowd has the causality backwards. I don't believe that the government forced lending institutions add more leverage than they wished to, or to do more aggressive lending than they wanted to. I think they were reacting to lobbying pressure from private industry itself. You see, private industry had found out that through CDOs they could magically turn BB subprime mortgages into AAA securities. What they needed was an open field to run with no government regulation. I believe the entire industry paid Congress to stand down and not regulate, and then hid their brazen lie of responsibility behind the clever phrase that they were all just trying to increase homeownership in America.

Similarly, Alan Greenspan is faulted for keeping interest rates at 1 percent for much too long a time and encouraging bubbles in the stock market and in the housing market. He supposedly ignored warnings from his regional advisors that fraudulent activity was occurring in the mortgage brokerage business, and that the mortgage terms were so crazy as to be unsustainable and the loans unrepairable.

Again, I don't see Alan Greenspan acting on the government's behalf, and certainly not on the behalf of the electorate. His economic philosophy throughout his life has been extremely libertarian. He is a major advocate of Ayn Rand. But he didn't develop this philosophy while in office; rather, he was appointed to office *because* he held this philosophy. The people didn't choose him; corporate controlled politicians selected him. Corporations put Alan Greenspan in office and corporations should take the blame for his policies. Alan Greenspan's economic philosophy was never mainstream and the American people never would have approved of it if they fully understood it. Thank goodness for Alan Greenspan that he spoke in unintelligible sentences.

So as to the question of who is more culpable, big business or big government, I can argue that big business is more culpable because they were the driving force, they were the ones spending money to influence Congress and the president, and it was their philosophy that was implemented. But on the other hand, Congress accepted the bribes. Congressmen knew exactly what they were doing when they took money from corporations in exchange for eliminating regulations. I sat on the Capitol steps in 1995 when Granny D., an eighty-nine-year-old widow from New Hampshire, finished her 3,000 mile walk across America protesting corporate lobbying and proclaimed in front of the Congress that they were a house of whores. It is difficult to assign more blame to the person who accepts the bribe than the one who pays it, but in this case it was Congress's express task to represent the people of the United States and so in taking bribes from corporations and enacting legislation favorable to those corporations, much of which harmed American citizens, they were not only thieves, but scoundrels, too. They violated their basic oath to the people.

Big business and big government share equal blame for the current mess. And I think the solution to this crisis and to providing a more stable economic environment in the world as we move forward is to figure out how to control both big business and big government. Too much free markets and big business runs rampant; too much regulation and big government takes over. I think the solution is in taking power away from both of them by insisting they both downsize into smaller, less powerful entities that are more controllable by the electorate, which will do much less damage if they fail to serve the people or their shareholders.

Lie #81 Government regulation is bad for economic growth and prosperity.

Another supposed truism in economics is that excessive government regulation is bad for a country's economic growth and prosperity. Imagine my surprise when the statistics work for a paper that Dick Roll and I wrote in 2002 showed that greater government expenditures in a country was correlated with greater country wealth—just the opposite of what traditional economics would have expected to find.

What the results of the study indicated was that bigger, more successful, wealthier and more developed countries typically had bigger governments as a percentage of GDP. Correlations such as this say nothing about the proper causality direction. It very well could be that more developed, richer countries grow for other reasons and then make a conscious decision to make their governments bigger. You could argue that this might be what happened in Europe, or even in the United States until recently. Capitalist and democratic institutions, including a strong rule of law and set of regulations, allowed these developed countries to grow rapidly and become wealthy. Once they had achieved substantial wealth, they then began to ask questions about how their less advantaged citizens were living. Many came to the conclusion that it was proper to increase the size of government to allow transfer payments from the well-off to the needy, the sick, the disabled and the elderly. Under this explanation, countries grow rich first and then decide to build big governments.

But the causality could just as well go the other direction. Maybe larger governments were helpful in building a successful economy. Until very recently, this statement would be taken as blasphemy at almost every major business school in the country. Almost every business school today teaches that government is the enemy of business and that government, with its unnecessary regulations, inhibits growth and prosperity.

But new academic work in the field of democratic and capitalist institutions demonstrates that government regulation and rule-making is a necessary component of any successful capitalist economic system. The free market and capitalism are based on rule-making. You cannot have a properly functioning free market without rules.

Libertarians, led by Milton Friedman, have gone so far as to suggest that the only proper role of government is national defense. Such a statement indicates to me that Friedman did not completely understand the foundations of the free market system he so revered, or maybe he had just learned to take them for granted. Certainly a Congress to enact laws that the people find necessary and reasonable and a court system to enforce those laws are essential ingredients in building a free market.

I believe that in his heart, Milton Friedman wrestled with the notion of whether democratically elected government should control the market and write regulations for it, or whether the free market should operate outside of government controls and mandates. His belief that governments often do wrong, even when they have good intentions, coupled with the fact that he didn't want anyone to interfere with what he saw as the beauty in the equilibrium of the free market, I think led him to mistakenly believe that free markets should operate outside of the purview of government regulation.

This is the mistake we have made for the last thirty years. We have allowed our financial markets and our commercial marketplace to become completely unregulated. We have assumed that the companies themselves would police their activities for fear of losing their good reputations—not realizing, of course, that hedge funds had no reputation to speak of, and could close up shop in a heartbeat if anything went wrong with their highly leveraged investments.

It will not be easy to fix this mistake. As we said, it extends not only from New York to Washington, DC, but to every Main Street in America. If you reinstitute regulation of commercial enterprise in America, you will be sad to find that much of our previous success is illusory. One of the reasons why our government has been slow to reregulate the financial industry is because the de-leveraging that will be involved, as well as the marking of assets to their true value, will cause many companies across the globe to become insolvent. There is no easy way out of this mess. There is going to be great pain involved. I can only hope that we take our medicine sooner rather than later and that we address the critical, fundamental problems in our capital markets and in our economy. Because of the enormous debts we face as a nation and the trillion-dollar-plus operating deficits we are running each year, we do not have unlimited time to fix these problems. It is critical that we make the correct decisions.

Lie #82 Rating agencies are regulated entities that work for investors to identify and price risk appropriately.

Of all the criminal behavior conducted by all the criminal participants in the schemes and scams that created the global credit crisis, I believe the most egregious was that conducted for profit by the rating agencies. The rating agencies' sole reason for existing is to evaluate risk. It is impossible to believe that risk evaluators at the rating agencies who had spent their entire careers in the mortgage securities markets would not ask fundamental questions about what would happen if housing prices declined in the future, and what this would mean for foreclosure default rates going forward.

Of course they knew to ask these questions. The fact that they didn't is evidence of their willful disregard for their purported mission: to evaluate risk. They were getting paid billions of dollars to label junk securities AAA. They were paid by issuers rather than investors, they participated in meetings in which the investment banks were structuring the securities and they accepted exorbitant fees. When the collapse came, they tried to argue that their ratings were not to be used to make investment decisions, but that their ratings were only their opinions, not about values, but about the securities' creditworthiness. And their opinions, they claim, were protected by their First Amendment rights.

Just as these companies reached a new low in accepting payment for higher ratings, certainly this explanation is a new low in defending wrongdoing. If this logic is accepted, it means that all fraudulent statements made during the sale of assets or securities can be protected under free speech rights. It is another example of these market participants believing that they are beyond the law and not subject to regulation. To claim that the Constitution gives them the right to say anything regarding a security's value is ludicrous.

Corporate clients who were about to issue new mortgage-backed securities would often approach one rating agency, and if they did not receive acceptable ratings, they would simply approach a second or third rating agency. It sounds very similar to how real estate agents hired appraisal firms to conduct supposedly "independent" appraisals of overvalued homes.

The major question for the markets now is how we go forward given that no one has any confidence in securities or companies' ratings. As I have said, investors grew to be so reliant on the rating agencies that they conducted very little of their own due diligence and investigation. The rug has literally been pulled out from under investors around the world. Do you think Klaus, the investment manager of the German bank I spoke of earlier, is capable of doing his own investment analysis of a complex CDO security? He wouldn't stand a chance. The math involved in analyzing a multi-tranche CDO with multiple classes of underlying assets such as mortgages, credit cards and student loans, with varying credit terms and originating from various locations and with risk spread unevenly across the tranches, is a task that has taken Wall Street decades to figure out. Based on their losses during the financial crisis, it doesn't look like even they were successful in completely understanding the risk.

This is another fundamental problem that must be addressed before we can have a successful recovery. What do we do about the fact that the rating agencies have not only lost all credibility, but that after they face the sustained lawsuits that are to come, they will probably have bankrupted themselves? In a world with no rating agencies, how will investors evaluate risk?

Lie #83 The SEC prevents insider trading and market manipulation.

The SEC has been charged with preventing insider trading and market manipulation. The fact of the matter is that the agency was basically told to stand down. Bush appointed a political crony, Christopher Cox, to head the agency. Since his appointment, the number of prosecutions that the SEC has raised for insider trading has dropped precipitously.

The evidence that is coming out now about the number of warnings the SEC received about the Bernie Madoff scandal is disheartening. One individual wrote six separate letters to the Boston and New York offices of the SEC, one of which was a seventeen-page description of why Madoff could not be achieving the returns he claimed through legal means.

The analysis was not overly complicated. It used simple arithmetic to show that if Bernie Madoff was indeed selling puts and calls in the S&P futures market, and he had a $17 billion portfolio to hedge, then his trading volume would have dwarfed the entire trading volume of that exchange for every day of the year.

I don't like it when, after a collapse or calamity, Monday morning quarterbacks go back and uncover damaging evidence that was ignored. After the fact, you know what type of evidence you are looking for. Before the fact, the evidence is just one of millions of pieces of evidence.

But in this case, it wasn't just that the evidence was available for the SEC to investigate; it was that the investigation had already been completed by a private citizen and handed to them. The SEC would have had to be complicit to not follow up on such an obvious claim. And what the newspapers refused to say in all of this, because it is so distasteful, is the simplest, most logical conclusion: the SEC wasn't just ignorant, they were complicit. Their lack of investigation and lack of prosecution makes them a co-conspirator in this financial fraud we call the credit crisis. Bush appointed people who were ill-prepared, and I am certain that the word was passed down that they were not looking for watchdogs to actively police the securities markets. Instead, the word went forth that no one would ever lose his job for lack of effort at pushing prosecutions, especially against well-connected types like Madoff.

The mainstream media has a tendency to report some pieces of the real story, but when the real story points toward big-time government corruption and complicity between Wall Street and big business, they never quite draw that conclusion. Most newspapers today are owned by big corporations, and I think the major reason they missed the big story is because journalists at these newspapers are close friends with the industry and government types they report on. Once you have covered a particular sector of the economy for a while as a journalist, I think you are much less likely to blow the whistle on your corporate and governmental drinking buddies.

Lie #84 Banks utilize off–balance sheet operations primarily to increase returns to their shareholders.

One of the lessons learned from the collapse of Enron was how important it was that corporations report all their activities and that they not be able to hide investment operations off–balance sheet. Enron used just about every trick in the book to get their assets off–balance sheet even though they actually continued to control those assets. Of course this improved their stated or reported return on assets as the earnings were captured by the parent company, but the assets never appeared on their books.

The fact that commercial banks utilized the same off–balance sheet techniques to hide assets from investors, leverage the amount of debt utilized in their operations, and dramatically increase returns to shareholders so quickly after Enron convinces me that Congress was not interested in any lessons learned from Enron.

It is unimaginable to me that we came out of Enron and passed the Sarbanes-Oxley Act, supposedly reformed the accounting profession so that such accounting irregularities would not occur in the future, and then just seven years later allowed the exact same off–balance sheet fiasco to occur again, this time in the commercial banking industry.

I must admit that I have not read the Sarbanes-Oxley legislation in detail. But I know it was passed by a Congress that was in the back pocket of industry. What was purported to be reform legislation likely has tremendous loopholes in it. Specifically, I will be shocked if the accounting firms allowed any tightening of their responsibility and liability to investors when they provide clean accounting statements to firms that quickly claim bankruptcy. If

the system is operating properly, one obvious result of this financial collapse—beyond the rating agencies simply going
bankrupt—is that every major accounting firm should also face
bankruptcy, given the large number of civil lawsuits that they
should face. But maybe they have received some sort of get-out-of-
jail-free card from Washington deep in the Sarbanes-Oxley
legislation.

Lie #85 Chinese walls within commercial and investment banks prevent conflicts of interest.

Chinese walls is a term—I'm honestly not sure where it came
from—that describes how investment banks and commercial
banks prevent their different areas of operations from causing conflicts of interest. You can imagine it would be quite discomforting
if there were not a Chinese wall between the investment bank's
merger department and their trading operations. The merger
department is continually exposed to nonpublic insider information about planned mergers and it would be a travesty if the
investment banks' trading departments found out about such
information and traded on it.

Similarly, there is a supposed Chinese wall between an investment
bank's research department and its investment banking division. The
research department is supposedly taking publicly available information, analyzing it, and making recommendations to the firm's
investing clients. The investment banking division advises major corporations and their executive managements, and because of this
often has in its possession very significant material nonpublic information such as company-generated forecasts and reports.

These Chinese walls are all self-regulating. There is no government official who comes in and sees that there is a physical wall
between the groups. Rather, it is just a culture of the firm that

grows and must be maintained to ensure that these conflicts of interest are not harmful to the company's clients.

But I believe, having spent nine years on Wall Street, that such Chinese walls are very porous. Even if the research analyst does not speak to the investment banking group, he reports to a senior person who heads up research. It is my belief that the senior executives often share information confidentially across departments.

It is hard to believe otherwise. The alternative explanation is that a very senior partner or executive in an investment bank has information derived from a confidential source that he knows will severely impact the value of securities the firm holds on a trading desk—and he does nothing about it. This is not in his interest or in his firm's interest. While such ethical action may be rewarded in heaven, I can ensure you it would be punished on Wall Street. If any investment bank lost $100 million on a position that they could have gotten out of if they had been warned by one of their own executives, that executive would not have much of a future with the firm.

Chinese walls are a classic example of why self-regulation doesn't work. Rules are written to satisfy government investigators and regulators, but there are always ways around rules. Without any law enforcement, laws become meaningless. Often, on Wall Street, the extent of enforcement is for a legal officer of the firm to make sure that the procedures are written down properly in the firm's policy handbook, and that every new employee receives a copy of that handbook. That may satisfy the loosely written procedures required by law, but it certainly opens up the opportunity to violate the intent of the law.

Lie #86 Excessive regulation is not needed in the financial markets because anyone who is harmed can seek redress in the courts.

A final argument for why regulation is not needed in the financial markets—and, for that matter, in any commercial market—is that anyone who is harmed always has the opportunity to seek redress in the court system.

This was Ronald Reagan's classic argument for why he believed less regulation was better. Numerous times he said that anybody who was harmed by a company ought to be able to seek redress. Only after Reagan's administration was successful in dismantling so much business regulation did future Republican administrations seek to limit the level of awards granted by juries in civil trials. The result was that someone could easily be harmed in an unregulated market, but if they sought redress in the court system, their compensation would be limited. It was the ideal world for big business. No regulation and a court system reduced to assigning meaningless parking tickets and fines instead of the reimbursement of actual losses suffered, including punitive damages awarded for deliberately egregious behavior.

In the financial markets, the story is even worse. It is the nature of the financial markets that all employee disputes and all client disputes go to a legal arbitrage system rather than directly to the US courts. All new employees and all new investing clients of a commercial or investment bank must sign an agreement saying that they will utilize arbitration rather than pursue recourse in a civil court for any harm they feel they have suffered at the hands of the investment bank or commercial bank.

What the employees and investing clients don't know is that the arbitrage system is controlled by Wall Street, and it very rarely finds against the Wall Street institutions or in favor of the employees and clients. Any award they do receive is limited to very reasonable fines or backpay. Such a system is Wall Street's own insurance system for preventing lawsuits against malpractice. Wall Street can do whatever they wish to their investing clients, but the clients never get their day in an open court of law.

Dealmakers on Wall Street have a similar insurance package against lawsuits. When structuring any merger deal or complex financial transaction, it is common practice that if you want to buy a company at $45 a share, you only offer $44 a share. The reason is that there is an entire industry of strike suit lawyers who automatically sue the investment bank and the acquirer, claiming that they are stealing the company. Then everything gets settled reasonably in talks between friends for a demand of just one more dollar per share. The company ends up getting acquired for $45, just as planned, but now the investment bank has been sued and settled, double indemnity is attached, and it is protected from any lawsuit claims in the future.

In this way, the investment banks have created a form of malpractice insurance that cost them nothing—the agreed-upon fee was going to be $45 to begin with. It is important for the suing lawyers to be able to claim to a judge that the price was pushed up by one dollar a share, which might work out to as much as $100 million, because they justify their fees as a percentage of this amount with the presiding judge. If they cannot point to some value they supposedly created for the *selling* shareholders, their fees are not allowed. The system works for everybody—except, of course, for a selling shareholder, who really is fraudulently taken out of his shares at an unfairly low price.

CHAPTER 12

The Real Reform Needed on Wall Street

Now that you have read through the biggest lies on Wall Street, you can see that there are many fundamental changes that must occur before our capital markets and our economy get straightened out. There is much lying and cheating going on in the system, both on Wall Street and in Washington, but very little progress will be made until the root causes of this crisis are uncovered and corrected.

Today, much of what has been tried to fix the economy has failed. I haven't liked any of the approaches taken to date at all.

Hank Paulson and George Bush originally said that they were going to be buying underwater mortgage securities from financial institutions as a way of freeing up capital for the banks. This made no sense to me because I did not see this as a liquidity crisis, but as a bank solvency crisis. Buying mortgages at discount prices from the banks would do nothing more than create additional losses for the banks, which would further threaten their solvency.

After Paulson woke up to this fact, he ended up not utilizing any of the TARP funds to buy underwater mortgages as he had promised Congress. Instead he turned around and gave $350 billion to some of his closest friends on Wall Street in the financial industry. In addition to these direct equity contributions and bailouts, he guaranteed $300 billion of Citigroup's assets. And all of this without asking debt investing in these companies to take a single dollar of losses.

Obama's announced stimulus plans also leave something to be desired. His combination of tax cuts and government spending means that the government will be spending an additional $800 billion. This means that the government deficit may approach $2.0 trillion in 2009.

A very simple explanation of what got us into this mess is that our citizens, our businesses, our banks and our government utilized a very low interest rate environment to dramatically increase borrowing and increase consumption. Now, both Bush and Obama plan on getting us out of this crisis by increasing debt to stimulate further consumption while holding interest rates near zero. This has to be the first time that the medicine given for an ailment is another heavy dose of exposure to whatever caused the illness in the first place. We can call the plan the hair of the dog; it reminds me of a drunk who has a drink first thing in the morning to try to cure his hangover.

The fact that almost all the economists in the world, regardless of their political persuasion or where they sit on the conservative/liberal spectrum, are supportive of Obama's big stimulus plan is not comforting. Rather, it makes me believe that all the economists have it wrong. I think they are all rehashing the same playbook that they all read in graduate school: $C + I + G = GDP$. They think that as C, consumption, goes down, GDP can be maintained by increasing G, government spending, or I, private investment. While their arithmetic is correct, I don't think it reflects the real world well at all.

If government spending could replace consumption in an economy, then all countries would do this. They would just have their governments increase spending whenever their GDP faltered. I can't think of a case where this has ever worked. FDR is credited by some for spending enormous amounts of money that helped us get out of the Great Depression, but other economists believe his emphasis on government spending prolonged the depression. For years, it was common knowledge that what really ended the Great Depression was government spending on WWII, but even now this assumption is being attacked by new academic research. It never made sense to me that it was economically productive to build tanks and bombs and planes for war so that you can go and destroy productive capacity in the world.

And what nobody is addressing is that we are not paying for this increase in government spending or for any tax cuts offered. We are borrowing the money and our children will have to pay it back. It is as if we are saying that we do not want to live with one dollar less of GDP, a bit less consumption, or a slightly different lifestyle from what we are used to, and in order to maintain our lifestyle we are willing to tax our children so that they will have to have a lower standard of living. It makes no sense.

A country cannot continue to borrow from its future generations forever. Somebody has to be willing to lend to that country. Especially in America, where the savings rate until just recently has been negative. The only way Obama and Bush's plan of implementing additional borrowing to fund even more unnecessary consumption will work is if foreign governments and foreign institutions continue to lend to the United States. It is not clear to me that they are going to forever.

George Bush came into office with a $5 trillion US debt, which itself had grown tremendously over the last thirty years. He went out of office with an $11 trillion debt, and this did not include $8 trillion of guarantees made by Hank Paulson and Ben Bernanke to try to stem the current crisis, or $5 trillion of questionable Fannie Mae and Freddie Mac assets the government has absorbed.

Even before any Obama stimulus plan or tax cut was taken into account, the Office of Management and Budget expected $1.2 trillion deficits in 2009. Layering on the Obama stimulus plan means that the deficit in 2009 could approach $2 trillion. Given that GDP is currently contracting from its high of $14 trillion, this means the operating deficit of our government may exceed 15 percent of our GDP. This will not only be the highest record level ever set, it will be the highest by a factor of two.

And, it doesn't count the biggest expenses of our government, namely Social Security and Medicare. It is estimated that unfunded liabilities for Medicare and Social Security will add another $35 trillion to the government's obligations, going forward on a present value basis.

If this recession continues for a number of years, one can easily see how the total government debt will quickly exceed $20 trillion and how the total liabilities of the government will exceed $50 trillion. Assuming that GDP shrinks into the $12 to $13 trillion range over the next few years, this means that our debt will be approaching four times our GDP.

This is an enormous number. It would put us in the category of the worst-capitalized, poorest developing countries of the world. Whether the United States has sufficient borrowing capacity to accomplish all of this government spending is no longer a hypothetical question. When our debt approaches these levels, foreign investors and foreign governments most certainly will pull back on their investments in America. China has recently announced that they are "worried" about their investments in US Treasury securities. If foreign countries and their largest institutions stop lending to America, the game is over. By running larger and larger annual operating deficits, we run the risk of not only increasing our debt to the point that foreigners revolt, but of creating an environment in which much of our government operations will have to shut down because the government will not have sufficient cash flow if its borrowing ability is taken away. We are running deficits and borrowing money to fund those deficits. This cannot go on for long.

I don't think we can borrow and spend our way out of this recession, and I'm especially suspicious of government spending, which has never been that productive in the past. How can borrowing a dollar from me so the government can spend it be considered a stimulus to the economy? Much of the trillion dollars that Obama plans to spend is going to go to the states because they are running shortfalls. They won't hire any new people. They will just continue to pay themselves rather high salaries relative to the private sector.

Another large chunk of the stimulus package will go to increasing and extending unemployment benefits. Again, an admirable cause, but it does nothing for creating new jobs.

Finally, the government is talking about creating new jobs to build highways, repair bridges, build wireless Internet access points in cities, invest in infrastructure, build electricity grids, and so on. Such large construction projects will provide work for day laborers, but very few Americans today are blue-collar construction workers. Almost all Americans today work in the service sector. It isn't like 1930, when creating jobs digging ditches helped out most Americans. Today construction jobs will help very few Americans. It's very difficult for the government to figure out a stimulus plan that will employ doctors, lawyers, bankers, and other professionals. That is why the private sector should create jobs, not government.

It would be much better than trying to artificially stimulate the economy to just allow the economy to contract. It had reached unsustainable levels because everybody was borrowing and consuming beyond their means. The economy needs to come back to a more reasonable level, just like house prices have to return to the reasonable level they were at before bank and mortgage lending went crazy.

If GDP were allowed to shrink back to 2002 levels, it wouldn't be the worst situation. Many of us were doing quite well in 2002. It doesn't mean that unemployment has to explode, but to the extent that productivity has improved, to achieve full employment we might each need to take a 5 to 10 percent haircut in our salaries. I think this would be an inexpensive way of getting us out of this crisis that otherwise threatens all of our jobs, our nation, and the world.

But companies, especially highly leveraged companies, cannot survive if GDP contracts. Their debt loads will push them into bankruptcy. This massive amount of debt our corporations and financial institutions have taken on is going to have to be dealt with one way or the other. I recommend creating a new bankruptcy court process that lasts for weeks rather than years so that companies can very quickly reorganize in bankruptcy and come out with better operating plans, new managements and less debt.

Another recommendation is to allow the government to inflate the currency and purposely cause substantial inflation—possibly as much as 20 percent inflation over the next couple of years. It sounds like a crazy idea, given how devastating inflation can be to an economy. But this is not a properly functioning economy. If you introduce substantial short-term inflation, everybody—consumers, the government businesses and the banks—will all see the real value of their debts decrease. This is what the world needs right now. Debtors need to be forgiven for a portion of the debt that they have taken on. Inflating the currency across the board does this quickly and efficiently and is appropriate since nearly everybody is over-leveraged. Assets around the world have dropped some $70 trillion, but the corresponding debt has not budged.

As I said, well into the second year of this recession, I cannot say that our government or the financial sector has developed an effective strategy for getting out. Throwing money at bankrupt firms in taxpayer bailouts before creditors took a single hit to their debt investments not only made no sense but was completely ineffective in slowing the weakening economy. Giving money outright to the largest financial institutions in the country may have staved off bankruptcy for those firms in the short run but, again, did too little to free up the credit markets or to increase lending to consumers and business.

President Obama's efforts to stimulate the economy by throwing money at Main Street through tax cuts to individuals and dramatic increases in government spending could easily fail. I don't think it will create enough jobs and I don't think it will slow the economy's decline.

So where are we then? In December 2009, we will be entering

the third year of the most serious global recession the world has seen in its history. There is a very real risk that it could become a depression if we continue to make mistakes in how we address the problem. Here, then, are the fundamental reforms I am recommending that must happen to stabilize our capital markets, to return confidence to our economy, and to fix our broken institutions.

First: we need not just greater transparency, but complete transparency of all assets, liabilities, guarantees, credit default swap exposures, and any other liabilities our corporations and our financial institutions are facing. I'm not talking about an extra two pages in an annual report. I'm talking about a disclosure that might extend to 1,000 pages and could be placed on the Internet for every company and financial institution in America. It is central that lenders, investors, creditors and business partners of companies and banks around the world completely understand where the risk resides in dealing with these individual companies.

Second: I would move for an immediate dissolution of the credit default swap market. Not only does the $65 trillion market bring enormous instability to the financial system, it has not been used as a hedging tool; instead, it is a purely speculative casino market.

In addition, the credit default swap market has created a level of interconnectedness between firms and the risks of their defaults such that capitalism and its theory of creative destruction is no longer able to operate. Because of their interconnectedness in the credit default swap market, almost every major firm in the country is too big to fail because they will trigger massive other failures in the system. Capitalism does not work when companies are too big to fail. It certainly doesn't work when almost all big companies and banks are too big to fail.

It seems extreme to want to shut down the entire CDS market, but it was a mistake from the beginning. Simply having a common clearinghouse for trades or introducing some meaningless and ineffective regulation does not eliminate the fundamental problem that massive sharing of default risk between firms creates a collectivism closer to socialism than capitalism. Capitalism is dependent on individual initiative and the ability for individual firms to compete and fail. The credit default swap market's sharing of default risk across all firms has nationalized default risk, not unlike a Third World dictator nationalizing the means of production.

I am praying that America is not fooled by the pundits and conservative columnists who tried to blame the current financial crisis solely on Washington and the government. Certainly, the government played a major role, but the primary reason for the crisis was deregulation. Yes, it was the government that deregulated business, but it was business that paid off the government through campaign contributions and lobbying efforts in order to become deregulated.

There is no way a free-market economy can work without regulation. It is a shame that we had to go through this enormous pain in order to see that. To many economists who have studied the importance of good institutions in creating economic growth, it was obvious that capitalism could not survive without proper rules, laws and regulation. Now hopefully we have all learned that lesson.

The challenge, of course, is for government to pass the right regulations. Again, as long as Wall Street and corporate America control our Congress through lobbying efforts, there is little hope that the meaningful regulations necessary to straighten out the markets will ever pass. Therefore, the third most fundamental change that has to happen, and possibly the most difficult to accomplish, is that all corporate lobbying and campaign contributions in Washington must end.

Next: there is way too much leverage throughout the system. Individuals are going to have to reduce their leverage by defaulting on their debts. But when they default, it creates a loss at the banking institution that lent money to them. These losses are going to threaten the solvency of our entire banking system and will require the entire banking system to recapitalize and restructure, hopefully through a quick bankruptcy process so that the bank creditors will have to suffer along with US taxpayers.

The banks themselves are overly leveraged. Their leverage ratios of 25 to 1 or 35 to 1 debt-to-equity need to come down to more reasonable levels like 8 to 1 or 12 to 1. For this to happen, the banks have to dramatically shrink their balance sheets. You can see how painful it is going to be on the global economy if all the banks of the world sell half of their assets and make no new loans. I don't see any way that we can avoid this pain and loss, and that is why I am so negative about the global economy's outlook for the next three to four years. This de-leveraging process is going to force governments, financial institutions, corporations, and consumers, to quit making new purchases that stimulate the economy and instead to use monies to pay down old debts. It is good business practice, but it means that the GDP will have to contract.

Fifth: we need to get rid of complexity for complexity's sake. Mortgages should all be thirty-year fixed rate with at least 10 percent downpayments. The derivatives market should be reexamined to see if its greater complexity is making the world safer or less stable.

Sixth: as we have seen in this text, there is a very serious principal agency problem in most of America's corporations and financial institutions. This needs to be seriously addressed. There are many middlemen in the investing process that also act as agents and do not necessarily have the investors' interests at heart. But the worst principal agent problem in the country right now is that management teams do not act with the shareholders' interests at heart. We must be smart enough to structure compensation agreements for management so that they are more perfectly aligned to think like shareholders. I believe this means that we cannot pay large cash bonuses, big stock options and restricted stock grants each year to managements. Such bonus compensation and stock ownership will have to be earned over time and not paid out for five to ten years. That is the only way I can see to get management to have the same long-term incentives as the shareholders. Management should not be motivated to grab quick profits that push up bonus pools and stock option values, but that threaten the long-term solvency of their firms. And we have to make sure that boards of directors represent shareholders, not management.

Seventh: after all these calls for regulation, you might conclude that I'm a big government liberal. Nothing could be further from the truth. I hate big government. I blame our education problems on the fact that government runs our primary and secondary schools. I think we fail in wars because our government runs them. I think our Social Security and Medicare systems are bankrupt because they are part of government. I can't think of a single thing the government does well. I believe our Congress is a house of whores and our presidency is often sold to the highest bidder.

So I have no respect for government, especially big government. This puts me in quite a dilemma. You see, I don't trust big business to operate without rules and regulations, but I don't think the government is smart enough or independent enough from big business to write effective rules. I think they will write rules, but I don't think they'll be the right ones, and I don't believe that the government will stay involved long enough to be sure they are implemented properly. George Stigler at the University of Chicago wrote his famous Nobel Prize–winning work showing that regulations do not hamper business, they help it. While the regulations are initially passed by activists interested in limiting business power, over time the activists lose interest and the businesses themselves take over the regulatory bodies and use them to minimize competition and maximize profits.

So I have a completely different solution to this entire problem than increasing the size and power of the government and having it write more regulations for business. I don't trust them to do it effectively.

My solution—which is radical, and at first you might find it hard to believe that we could accomplish it—is to downsize everything. Make everything smaller and less concentrated in power. Power corrupts and absolute power corrupts absolutely. We need to figure out a way in which the federal government is not so large and powerful that it can dictate terms to its own people and make them feel as if they are the slaves of their government instead of the government being the servants of the people. I believe this can be accomplished through a series of initiatives such as a greater emphasis on direct voting rather than representative voting, more emphasis on frequent polling of citizens, and dramatically limiting the length of service of congressmen and senators in Washington.

Similarly, we need to limit the power of corporations that have gotten to be too big and too powerful. My suggestion is that every time a company becomes larger than $100 billion in market capitalization, including its debt, or attains greater than $300 billion in assets, the company should be broken up into two or three new companies. There is no dissolution of value because each old shareholder would receive shares in each of the two or three new companies. But companies would not be allowed to grow to such a size that they can dictate terms to government or develop monopoly positions in the marketplace. I know it sounds extremely radical, but it is the basis of how capitalism is supposed to work. Capitalism assumes that the agents participating in the market are completely independent and small enough that they cannot have an influence over the marketplace or over the regulations of the marketplace. Our largest banks and corporations clearly violate this basic tenet of capitalism.

I think putting the restriction on the size of companies—and it would need to be done globally through negotiations with other countries—would unleash a dramatic increase in entrepreneurship and innovation in this country. Could you imagine if, rather than just having three auto companies, thirty or forty years ago we had broken the Big Three in Detroit up into nine auto companies? I think that by now under this formula we would have had twenty to thirty automobile companies, each of them continually innovating and creating new products such as hybrid vehicles, hydrogen vehicles, and electric vehicles. This type of innovation will happen in every industry naturally once we break very large companies up and prevent their muscle from allowing healthy innovation by smaller competitors.

That is my short list of the reforms I would like to see accomplished. I understand that these are major reforms, but you understand that this is a major crisis. We have come as close as any time in our lifetimes to a complete collapse of the global financial system and the world economy. I suggest that we not try this again. We need to accomplish these major changes to the way our capital markets and government are organized to ensure that this never happens again.

My outlook for the economy, as you can imagine, is not optimistic. As I said, I don't believe Obama will be successful in spending our way out of this recession. I also think this recession is far different than any short recession we have had in the past because of the tremendous leverage in the system that needs to be reduced and because of the structural problems in the way our capital markets are regulated that need to be addressed. We need to fundamentally change the way big business and big government work in this country. This crash has proved that the current system does not work and that minor adjustments will not help.

My prediction is that the economy will continue to trend downward for a number of years, not months. And rather than bouncing back as in past recessions, I believe that for a long period of time, five to eight years, the economy will struggle at a low level of output. The recovery will not be a V-shaped recovery, in which there is an instant bounce back, but more of an L recovery, in which we trade down and stay at a low output level for a long period of time.

There is also the very real risk, even though at this time it might be only 20 or 25 percent, that these warnings will be ignored, that Congress will continue to do the bidding of big corporations, that the American people will lose confidence in their financial markets and their government and that the entire system will collapse and we will head into a very real depression. Under this scenario there is no limit to how bad things might get. As I said earlier, I believe some 25 percent of Americans are already unemployed, and this number could grow to 35 or 40 percent in a depression scenario.

If you are looking for stock price predictions, that is more difficult. I will say this. At 7,000 to 8,000, the stock market certainly has more downside than upside. It looks like the S&P 500 is going to earn approximately $50 in 2009, and if you assign a ten multiple to that, that gets you to an S&P valuation of 500. That is a further decline of about 35 percent from where the S&P is now. I cannot think of any upside scenario for stocks other than that they might temporarily improve under an Obama stimulus plan, but it will only be temporary.

I think that debt markets are certain to deteriorate. It makes no sense that a country with as much debt as the United States and with its trillions of dollars of annual operating deficits is able to borrow money at interest rates near zero percent. These rates that the US needs to pay in order to borrow funds are going to increase dramatically because inflation is going to come back. Inflation has to come back because the government will be printing money to fund all of these programs when people refuse to lend to us. When inflation comes back, interest rates will spike, and those 2 percent ten-year Treasury bonds you bought will be worth about $.50 on the dollar.

While I believe commodity prices will continue to stay low, they will also increase in price as inflation returns. I would not recommend holding commodities because the real demand for them will decline as the economy softens, but the nominal price may increase as inflation reignites. The only place I would seek shelter from the storm with your investment funds is in gold and TIPS. Both of them will be good long-term protectors of your purchasing power, as they both do a very good job protecting against unexpected inflation.

As for housing prices, I believe they still have two or three more years to head down, and they will not recover back to where they were. There is no way banks will be lending ten times your income for you to buy a house with no money down. Those days are gone. Under new, saner lending requirements and qualifications, housing prices will have to come down at least 30 percent nationwide from their peaks and more than 50 to 60 percent on the coasts, in California and Florida, and in Las Vegas and Arizona.

It has not been easy writing a book completely about lying. There were days during the writing of this book when the subject matter depressed me so much that I had to stop and take a break. I find it enormously disturbing that Americans, and now citizens of the world, are suffering very real hardships from a crisis that could easily have been avoided but for the lies of Wall Street, our biggest corporations, and our government. It is estimated that an additional 200,000 to 400,000 babies in the world will die of malnutrition solely because of the malfeasance of big business and our government.

In closing, I know that we will never be successful in ending all lies. So my only advice is to be extremely careful who you trust. In financial dealings, always ask the question: what does this person who is advising me have to gain? Always try to understand what philosophical school the person comes from. If someone is an ardent libertarian, it doesn't make any difference what the facts are: they are going to suggest a solution that involves less government involvement. If you can identify their biases in advance, it will help you understand their advice.

My very strong advice is to not accept lying in your personal and professional lives going forward. I believe that as a society, we have been much too forgiving of people who lie to us and cheat us. It will not stop until we make it so. Do not let liars and cheaters off the hook. Publicly call them on their unethical behavior and embarrass them. If it involves financial dealings, arrest them. But do not let them get away with it.

Truthfulness is not only the foundation of our society and a strong economic system, it is the basis of all human interaction and organization, and without it life can seem purposeless and unfulfilling.

And now the hardest advice of all. Let us stop lying to each other. Lying is not a victimless crime. Lying causes real suffering and hardship. Let's do all we can to make our lives a search for the truth, and in so doing truly inspire others to lead more fulfilling and ethical lives.

Index

Afghanistan, war in, 16
American Bankers Association, 28
Argentina, 147–148
Asian flu, 18
auto industry, 59–60

bail out, 52–54, 59–60, 226
banking system, 36, 37, 50–51
bankruptcy, 47, 49, 51, 181, 225
Bear Stearns, 52, 60
Bernanke, Ben, 48, 55, 84, 223
bonds, 83–85, 109–112
    tax-free municipal, 112–114
    Treasury Inflation-Protected
        Securities (TIPS), 74–75,
        105–107
    US Treasuries, 103–114, 127
Buffett, Warren, 55
Bush, George, 134, 142–146, 221,
    222–223
business cycles, 140–142

campaign contributions, 6, 23, 29,
    42
capitalism, 35–38, 175–178
Cerberus, 53
China, 133, 177–180
Chinese walls, 217–218
Citigroup, 9, 10, 221
Clinton, Bill, 142–143, 145, 188, 191
collateralized debt obligations
    (CDOs), 19, 22
commercial banks, 27, 40, 45–47,
    60, 138–140, 158
commodities, 63, 122–124
Community Reinvestment Act
    (CRA), 21, 207
Cramer, Jim, 75, 81, 88

credit cards, 25
credit default swaps, 58, 68,
    186–188, 192, 194, 195, 227

debt leverage, 157–159
defense spending, 17
deflation, 106, 135–136
deregulation, 5, 6, 28, 228
derivatives, 188–195, 197-198
diversification, 7, 38–41, 63–69
dollar cost averaging, 75–76
Dow Jones Industrial Average, 15
Drexel Burnham, 163–164

Earnings before interest taxes and
    depreciation and amortization
    (EBITDA), 91–92
elderly citizens, 149–151
European economic model, 182–183
executive compensation, 53, 54,
    160–161

fairness, 3, 4
Fama, Eugene, 49
Fannie Mae, 12, 22–23, 28, 52, 53,
    61, 194, 207–208, 223
Federal Reserve, 48, 49, 52, 85,
    107–109, 135, 137–139, 140–141,
    189
financial advisors, 80–82, 88–90,
    109, 133
foreclosure, 11
fraud, 5
Freddie Mac, 12, 22–23, 28, 52, 53,
    61, 194, 207–208, 223
Friedman, Milton, 76, 88, 144, 211
fund of funds, 197–198

General Motors (GM), 30, 52
globalization, 17, 30, 43, 98,
    167–169, 177, 180–181, 183
GMAC, 52, 53, 55, 60, 62
gold, 74–75, 126–128
Goldman Sachs, 52, 55, 56, 60, 62,
    91, 190
Great Depression, 48, 71
Greenspan, Alan, 26, 38, 137–139,
    191, 208
Gross Domestic Product (GDP), 15,
    16, 17, 134–136, 151–153, 223

health care, 16, 44, 59, 60, 72–73,
    77, 92, 100, 113, 133, 143, 147,
    182
hedge funds, 8, 29, 82, 195–198,
    200–206
housing market, 10, 11, 87, 124–126,
    194
Hunt, Bunky, 123

illegal immigrants, 15, 134
India, 178–180
inflation, 85, 95, 99–100, 105, 106,
    110, 126, 134, 136–137
insider trading, 214–216, 217
insurance business, 37
interest rates, 95, 107–109, 138, 141
international lending, 8
international trade, 171–173
Iraq, war in, 16

J.P. Morgan, 52, 56, 191, 194
Japan (real estate crisis), 17, 47, 51
job growth, 142–143
junk bonds, 163–164
junk bond credit spreads, 9
justice, 3, 4

Laffer, Art, 143–146
laissez-faire, 5

Lehman Brothers, 60, 190
leverage buyout, 8
life-cycle investing, 76–78
lobbying, 6, 42–44, 175, 228
long-lived asset and liability
    business, 37, 38

Madoff, Bernie, 198–200, 214–215
Medicare, 16, 24, 84, 114, 224, 230
mergers, 165–166
Merrill Lynch, 52, 190
Mexico, 18
Milken, Michael, 163
Modigliani (Franco), 95–96
money supply, 48, 135–136, 139
monopoly power, 5
Morgan Stanley, 52, 56, 60, 190
Mortgage Bankers Association, 28
mortgage securities, 164–165

National Association of Realtors, 28
natural resource wealth, 169–171
    Africa, 170–171
    China, 171
    Middle East, 170
Northern Rock, 62

Obama, Barack, 134, 222–226
    stimulus plan of, 134, 145, 221,
    225–226

P/E ratios, 100–102
Paulson, Henry, 49, 54–57, 84, 165,
    190, 208, 221, 223
pollution, 16, 17
Ponzi scheme, 199–200
population growth, 15
preferred shares, 128–130
    convertible, 129–130
prime borrowers, 20
private equity firms, 115–117

Rand, Ayn, 26, 209
rating agencies, 8, 27, 32–35, 40,
    64, 212–214
Reagan, Ronald, 5, 28, 100, 143–145,
    219
recession, 18, 24, 71, 85, 123, 124,
    133–134, 138, 140, 178–180,
    224
regulation, 4, 26, 29, 167–168, 188,
    207–210, 212, 219–220
risk management, 10, 11
Roll, Dick, 172, 176, 210
Rubin, Robert, 145, 188, 191
rule of law, 3, 29, 90, 210
Russia, 18

Saudi Arabia, 123
SEC, 214–216
Senate Banking Committee, 6
Smith, Adam, 39
Social Security, 16, 24, 77, 78, 84,
    114, 149–151, 224, 230
Stigler, George, 230
stock options, 32, 117–120
subprime mortgages, 7, 8, 18–28, 45
Summers, Lawrence, 188

tax cuts, 143–146
too big to fail, 57-58, 227
trade deficit, 17
Treasury Department, 49
Treasury Inflation-Protected
    Securities (TIPS), 74–75,
    105–107
Treasury securities, very short-term,
    74–75
Troubled Assets Relief Program
    (TARP), 49, 54–56, 165, 221

unemployment, 131–134, 136
unions, 17

venture capital funds, 120–122
Volcker, Paul, 144

wages, 99, 136–137
Warren, Elizabeth, 56
wealth, 146–148
    redistribution of, 173–175
Welch, Jack, 89
World Trade Organization (WTO),
    167–168

ABOUT THE AUTHOR

A former investment banker for Goldman Sachs and previously a Visiting Scholar at UCLA's Anderson School of Management, John R. Talbott is the author of seven books on economics and politics, including, most recently, *Obamanomics: How Bottom-Up Economic Prosperity Will Replace Trickle-Down Economics* and *Contagion: The Financial Epidemic That Is Sweeping the Global Economy . . . and How to Protect Yourself from It*. His other books include *The Coming Crash in the Housing Market* and *Sell Now! The End of the Housing Bubble*. He has written for the *Wall Street Journal*, the *Financial Times*, the *Boston Globe*, the *San Francisco Chronicle*, the *Herald Tribune*, the *New Republic*, and appeared as a commentator on CNN, Fox, CNBC, FBN, CBS, and MSNBC.